ENCYCLOPÆDIA
Britannica®

10-Minute Guide
U.S. HISTORY

Publications International, Ltd.

Louis Weber, CEO
Publications International, Ltd.
8140 Lehigh Avenue
Morton Grove, IL 60053

ISBN: 978-1-68022-877-9

Manufactured in China.

8 7 6 5 4 3 2 1

TABLE OF CONTENTS

The United States of AMERICA

The United States
is the fourth largest country in the world in area
(after Russia, Canada, and China).

The major characteristic of the United States is probably its great variety. Its physical environment ranges from the Arctic to the subtropical, from the moist rain forest to the arid desert, from the rugged mountain peak to the flat prairie. Although the total population of the United States is large by world standards, its overall population density is relatively low. The country embraces some of the world's largest urban concentrations as well as some of the most extensive areas that are almost devoid of habitation.

The United States contains a highly diverse population. Unlike a country such as China that largely incorporated indigenous peoples, the United States has a diversity that to a great degree has come from an immense and sustained global immigration. Probably no other country has a wider range of racial, ethnic, and cultural types than does the United States. In addition to the presence of surviving Native Americans (including American Indians, Aleuts, and Eskimos) and the descendants of Africans taken as slaves to the New World, the national character has been enriched, tested, and constantly redefined by the tens of millions of immigrants who by and large have come to America hoping for greater social, political, and economic opportunities than they had in the places they left.

Growth and Prosperity

The United States is the world's greatest economic power, measured in terms of gross domestic product (GDP). The nation's wealth is partly a reflection of its rich natural resources and its enormous agricultural output, but it owes more to the country's highly developed industry.

Despite its relative economic self-sufficiency in many areas, the United States is the most important single factor in world trade by virtue of the sheer size of its economy. Its exports and imports represent major proportions of the world total. The United States also impinges on the global economy as a source of and as a destination for investment capital.

The major regions of the U.S.—the Interior Lowlands and their upland fringes, the Appalachian Mountain system, the Atlantic Plain, the Western Cordillera, and the Western Intermontane Region—are so various that they require further division into 24 major subregions, or provinces.

The Land

The center of the conterminous United States is a great sprawling interior lowland, reaching from the ancient shield of central Canada on the north to the Gulf of Mexico on the south. To east and west this lowland rises, first gradually and then abruptly, to mountain ranges that divide it from the sea on both sides. The two mountain systems differ drastically. The Appalachian Mountains on the east are low, almost unbroken, and in the main set well back from the Atlantic. From New York to the Mexican border stretches the low Coastal Plain, which faces the ocean along a swampy, convoluted coast. The gently sloping surface of the plain extends out beneath the sea, where it forms the continental shelf, which, although submerged beneath shallow ocean water, is geologically identical to the Coastal Plain. Southward the plain grows wider, swinging westward in Georgia and Alabama to truncate the Appalachians along their southern extremity and separate the interior lowland from the Gulf.

West of the Central Lowland is the mighty Cordillera, part of a global mountain system that rings the Pacific basin. The Cordillera encompasses fully one-third of the United States, with an internal variety commensurate with its size. At its eastern margin lie the Rocky Mountains, a high, diverse, and discontinuous chain that stretches all the way from New Mexico to the Canadian border. The Cordillera's western edge is a Pacific coastal chain of rugged mountains and inland valleys, the whole rising spectacularly from the sea without benefit of a coastal plain. Pent between the Rockies and the Pacific chain is a vast intermontane complex of basins, plateaus, and isolated ranges so large and remarkable that they merit recognition as a region separate from the Cordillera itself.

The United States still offers its residents opportunities for unparalleled personal advancement and wealth. However, the depletion of its resources, the contamination of its environment, and the continuing social and economic inequality that perpetuates areas of poverty and blight all threaten the fabric of the country.

AMERICA
Before European Colonization

Until the late 1980s, it was generally believed—on the basis of evidence of the Clovis projectile points that had been found in New Mexico—that humans arrived in the Americas approximately 13,500 years ago. During the last ice age, a "land bridge" (a misnomer for a very broad swath of land) connected northeastern Asia to northwestern North America. The land route is known as Beringia because it formed along the present-day Bering Strait. Beringia began to emerge some 36,000–40,000 years ago, as the ice age began. At that time glaciers began to absorb increasing amounts of water, causing global sea levels to fall by as much as 400 feet (120 meters). A complete connection between Asia and North America existed about 28,000–10,000 BCE, and, at its greatest extent, Beringia may have spanned some 1,000 miles (1,600 km) from north to south. The people who moved into Beringia from Asia relied on hunting and gathering for subsistence and traveled in bands: small, mobile, kin-based groups of people who lived and foraged together.

By about 6000 BCE, some groups had begun to experiment with food production as well as foraging; they are known as Archaic cultures. Archaic peoples often returned to the same location on a seasonal basis, and as a result began to build small settlements. Archaic subsistence techniques were very efficient, and in a number of culture areas people sustained an essentially Archaic way of life until after European colonization.

The Clovis and Folsom Cultures

In 1908 George McJunkin, ranch foreman and former slave, reported that the bones of an extinct form of giant bison (*Bison antiquus*) were eroding out in a wash near Folsom, New Mexico; an ancient spear point was later found embedded in the animal's skeleton. In 1929 teenager Ridgley Whiteman found a similar site near Clovis, New Mexico, albeit with mammoth rather than bison remains. The Folsom and Clovis sites yielded the first indisputable evidence that ancient Americans had co-existed with and hunted the megafauna, a possibility that most scholars had previously met with skepticism.

The Clovis culture proved to be the earlier of the two. Clovis projectile points are thin, lanceolate (leaf-shaped), and made of stone; one or more longitudinal flakes, or flutes, were removed from the base of each of the point's two flat faces. Clovis culture was long believed to have lasted approximately 9500–9000 BCE, although early 21st-century analyses suggest it may have been of shorter duration, approximately 9050–8800 BCE. Folsom culture seems to have developed from Clovis culture. Also lanceolate, Folsom points were more carefully manufactured and include much larger flutes than those made by the Clovis people. The Lindenmeier site, a Folsom campsite in northeastern Colorado, has yielded a wide variety of end and side scrapers, gravers (used to engrave bone or wood), and bone artifacts. The Folsom culture is thought to have lasted approximately 9000–8000 BCE. Related Paleo-Indian groups, such as the Plano culture, persisted until sometime between 6000–4000 BCE.

Associated with Clovis are such implements as bone tools, hammer-stones, scrapers, and projectile points. The typical Clovis point is leaf-shaped, with parallel or slightly convex sides and a concave base. The edges of the basal portions are ground somewhat, probably to prevent the edge from severing the hafting cord. Clovis points range in length from 1.5 to 5 inches (4 to 13 centimeters) and are heavy and fluted, though the fluting rarely exceeds half the length. Some eastern variants of Clovis—called Ohio, Cumberland, or Suwannee, depending on their origin—are somewhat fish-tailed and also narrower relative to length.

Many prehistoric Native American peoples eventually adopted some degree of agriculture; they are said to have transitioned from the Archaic to subsequent culture periods when evidence indicates that they began to rely substantively upon domesticated foods and in most cases to make pottery. Archaeologists typically place the end of the North American Archaic at or near 1000 BCE, although there is substantial regional variation from this date.

Archaic Cultures

Beginning about 6000 BCE, what had been a relatively cool and moist climate gradually became warmer and drier. A number of cultural changes are associated with this environmental shift; most notably, bands became larger and somewhat more sedentary, tending to forage from seasonal camps rather than roaming across the entire landscape. Fish, fowl, and wild plant

foods (especially seeds) also become more apparent in the archaeological record, although this may be a result of differential preservation rather than changes in ancient subsistence strategies. Finally, various forms of evidence indicate that humans were influencing the growth patterns and reproduction of plants through practices such as the setting of controlled fires to clear forest underbrush, thereby increasing the number and productivity of nut-bearing trees.

The Plains Archaic continued until approximately the beginning of the Common Era, and other groups maintained an essentially Archaic lifestyle well into the 19th century, particularly in the diverse microenvironments of the Pacific Coast, the arid Great Basin, and the cold boreal forests, tundra, and coasts of Alaska and Canada.

AMERICA
Before European Colonization

In much of North America, the shift from generalized foraging and horticultural experimentation to a way of life dependent on domesticated plants ocurred about 1000 BCE, although regional variation from this date is common.

Corn (maize), early forms of which had been grown in Mexico since at least 5000 BCE, appeared among Archaic groups in the Southwest culture area by about 1200 BCE and in the Eastern Woodlands by perhaps 100 BCE; other Mesoamerican domesticates, such as chile peppers and cotton, did not appear in either region until approximately the beginning of the Common Era.

Although the importance of these foreign domesticates increased over time, most Native American groups retained the use of locally domesticated plants for several centuries.

Southwestern Cultures

The first centuries of the Common Era saw the development of three major farming complexes in the Southwest, all of which relied to some extent on irrigation. The Ancestral Pueblo peoples (also known as the Anasazi; c.100–1600 CE) of the Four Corners area built low walls (check dams) to slow and divert the flow of water from seasonal rivulets to cultivated fields. The Mogollon (c. 200–1450 CE) built their communities in the mountainous belt of southwestern New Mexico and southeastern Arizona and depended upon rainfall and stream diversion to water their crops. The Hohokam (c. 200–1400 CE) lived in the desert area of the Gila basin of southern Arizona and built irrigation canals to water their fields.

Although earlier Ancestral Puebloan villages were built in the open, the people began to build cliff dwellings around 1150, perhaps as a defense against invading groups of ancestral Navajo and Apache. In addition to the natural protection provided by a cliff, the absence of doors and windows to the rooms on the ground floor left a solid outer stone wall that could be surmounted only by climbing a ladder; ladders could easily be removed if the town were attacked.

Pueblo architecture is a traditional style of architecture of the Pueblo Indians of the southwestern United States. The multistoried, permanent, attached homes typical of this tradition are modeled after the cliff dwellings built by the Ancestral Pueblo (Anasazi) culture. This architectural form continued to be used by many Pueblo peoples in the early 21st century.

These three cultures are known for their geographic expansion, population growth, and pueblo architecture, all of which reached their greatest levels of complexity between approximately 700 and 1300—a period that generally coincided with an unusually favorable distribution of rainfall over the entire Southwest (analogous climatic conditions elsewhere in North America supported cultural florescences in the Eastern Woodlands [c. 700–1200] and on the Plains [c. 1000–1250]). During this period the population and cultures of central and western Mexico expanded to the northwest; trade and cultural stimuli were thus moving from Mesoamerica into the Southwest culture area at a time when the climate in both regions was most favorable for population and cultural growth. Materials entering the Southwest from Mexico during this era included cast copper bells, parrots, ball courts, shell trumpets, and pottery with innovative vessel shapes and designs.

Mississippian Cultures

The Mississippian cultural complex originated in the Mississippi valley between what are now St. Louis, Mo., and Vicksburg, Miss., and developed from local traditions. Between 700 and 1000 CE small Eastern Woodland villages grew into large towns with subsidiary villages and farming communities nearby. Regionally delimited styles of pottery, projectile points, house types, and other utilitarian products reflected diverse ethnic identities. Notably, however, Mississippian peoples were also united by two factors that cross-cut ethnicity: a common economy that emphasized corn production and a common religion focusing on the veneration of the sun and a variety of ancestral figures.

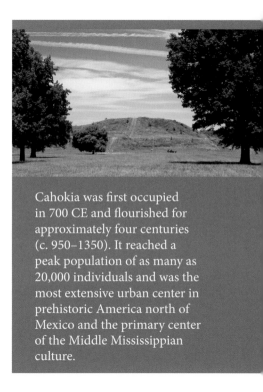

Cahokia was first occupied in 700 CE and flourished for approximately four centuries (c. 950–1350). It reached a peak population of as many as 20,000 individuals and was the most extensive urban center in prehistoric America north of Mexico and the primary center of the Middle Mississippian culture.

One of the most outstanding features of Mississippian culture was the earthen temple mounds. These mounds often rose to a height of several stories and were capped by a flat area, or platform, on which were placed the most important community buildings—council houses and temples.

Cahokia

Cahokia Mounds, in southwestern Illinois, originally consisted of about 120 mounds spread over 6 square miles (16 square km), but some of the mounds and other ancient features have been destroyed. The site and its hinterland declined and were eventually abandoned, probably because of environmental degradation, although it has been suggested that disease, climatic change, societal stress, and warfare may have been contributing factors. The population placed substantial demands on wood resources for fuel and construction and, during the initial centuries of the city's occupation, cleared the forests upstream of the site. The denuded watershed produced greatly increased rates of runoff, erosion, and unseasonable summer flooding in Cahokia's fields, causing crops to fail and overall production to decline. The economic and social consequences were disastrous, probably leading to starvation, loss of faith in leadership, increased competition for land, and regional warfare.

EUROPEAN
Exploration and Expansion

In the hundred years from the mid-15th to the mid-16th century, a combination of circumstances stimulated men to seek new routes to the East; and it was new routes rather than new lands that filled the minds of kings and commoners, scholars and seamen. First, toward the end of the 14th century, the vast empire of the Mongols was breaking up; thus, Western merchants could no longer be assured of safe-conduct along the land routes. Second, the growing power of the Ottoman Turks, who were hostile to Christians, blocked yet more firmly the outlets to the Mediterranean of the ancient sea routes from the East. Third, new nations on the Atlantic shores of Europe were now ready to seek overseas trade and adventure.

Columbus's tenacity, courage, and skill in navigation make him stand out among the few explorers who have substantially changed ideas about the world. Did he believe to the end that he indeed had reached Cathay, or did he, however dimly, perceive that he had found a New World?

Christopher Columbus

It is not known when the idea originated of sailing westward in order to reach Cathay (China). Many sailors set forth searching for islands in the west; and it was a commonplace among scientists that the East could be reached by sailing west, but to believe this a practicable voyage was an entirely different matter. Christopher Columbus, a Genoese who had settled in Lisbon about 1476, argued that Cipango (Japan) lay a mere 2,500 nautical miles west of the Canary Islands in the eastern Atlantic. He took 45 instead of 60 nautical miles as the value of a degree; he accepted Ptolemy's exaggerated west–east extent of Asia and then added to it the lands described by Marco Polo, thus reducing the true distance between the Canaries and Cipango by about one-third. He could not convince the Portuguese scientists nor the merchants of Lisbon that his idea was worth backing; but eventually he obtained the support of King Ferdinand and Queen Isabella of Spain.

On August 3, 1492, Columbus sailed from Palos, Spain, with three small ships manned by Spaniards. From the Canaries he sailed westward, for, on the evidence of the globes and maps in which he had faith, Japan was on the same latitude. If Japan should be missed, Columbus thought that the route adopted would land him, only a little further on, on the coast of China itself. Fair winds favored him, the sea was calm, and, on October 12, landfall was made on the Bahama island of Guanahaní, which he renamed San Salvador. With the help of the local Indians, the ships reached Cuba and then Haiti. Although there was no sign of the wealth of the lands of Kublai Khan, Columbus nevertheless seemed convinced that he had reached China, since, according to his reckoning, he was beyond Japan.

A second voyage in 1493 and 1494, searching fruitlessly for the court of Kublai Khan, further explored the islands of "the Indies." On his third voyage, in 1498, Columbus sighted Trinidad, entered the Gulf of Paria, on the coast of what is now Venezuela, and annexed for Spain "a very great continent . . . until today unknown." On a fourth voyage, from 1502 to 1504, he explored the coast of Central America from Honduras to Darien on the Isthmus of Panama, seeking a navigable passage to the west.

Ferdinand Magellan

Ferdinand Magellan had served in the East Indies as a young man. Familiar with the long sea route to Asia eastward from Europe via the Cape of Good Hope, he was convinced that there must be an easier sea route westward. His plan was in accord with Spanish hopes; five Spanish ships were fitted out in Sevilla, and in August 1519 they sailed under his command first to the Cape Verde Islands and thence to Brazil. Standing offshore, they then sailed southward along the east coast of South America; the estuary of the Río de la Plata was explored in the vain hope that it might prove to be a strait leading to the Pacific. Magellan's ships then sailed south along the coast of Patagonia.

In September 1520 a southward course was set once more, until, finally, on October 21, Magellan found a strait (now named the Strait of Magellan) at the southern tip of South America that led westward. It proved to be an extremely difficult one: it was long, deep, tortuous, rock-walled, and bedeviled by icy squalls and dense fogs. It was a miracle that three of the five ships got through its 325-mile length. After 38 days, they sailed out into the open ocean. The Pacific proved to be of vast extent, and for 14 weeks the little ships sailed on a northwesterly course without encountering land. Short of food and water, the sailors ate sawdust mixed with ship's biscuits and chewed the leather parts of their gear to keep themselves alive. At last, on March 6, 1521, exhausted and scurvy-ridden, they landed at the island of Guam. Ten days later they reached the Philippines, where Magellan was killed in a local quarrel. The survivors, in two ships, sailed on to the Moluccas; thus, sailing westward, they arrived at last in territory already known to the Portuguese sailing eastward.

Ferdinand Magellan. From Spain he sailed around South America, discovering the Strait of Magellan, and across the Pacific. Though he was killed in the Philippines, one of his ships continued westward to Spain, accomplishing the first circumnavigation of Earth.

EUROPEAN SETTLEMENTS
in the New World

New France

The name Gallia Nova (New France) was first recorded in 1529 on a map prepared by the brother of Giovanni da Verrazano, who, in the service of France, had explored the coasts of North America in 1524 from what is now the Carolinas north to Nova Scotia. Then in 1534, the French navigator and explorer Jacques Cartier entered the Gulf of St. Lawrence and took possession of New France for King Francis I. In succeeding years Cartier ascended the St. Lawrence as far as the Lachine Rapids, to where Montreal now stands, and attempted, with Jean-François de La Rocque, sieur de (lord of) Roberval, to found a colony near what is now Quebec. The colony failed, but out of these explorations the French fur trade with the Native Americans (First Nations) of the gulf and the river regions began. Samuel de Champlain was employed in the interests of successive fur-trading monopolies and sailed into the St. Lawrence in 1603. In the next year, he was on the Bay of Fundy and had a share in founding the first French colony in North America—that of Port-Royal, (now Annapolis Royal, Nova Scotia). In 1608 he began the settlement that was named Quebec, selecting a commanding site that controlled the narrowing of the St. Lawrence River estuary.

The Spanish in the Caribbean

When Columbus returned to Spain from his voyage of 1492, having hit upon the island of Hispaniola (now divided between the Dominican Republic and Haiti) as his base, his concept of what should be done thereafter was in the Italian-Portuguese maritime tradition. He wanted to explore further for trading partners, and he considered all who came along with him to be employees of an enterprise headed by himself. The Spaniards, however, immediately started moving in the direction of their own traditions. The expedition that returned to Hispaniola in 1493 was far more elaborate than it needed to have been for Columbus' purposes, containing a large number and variety of people, animals, and equipment for a large-scale, permanent occupation of the island.

Santo Domingo (located on the island of Hispaniola and founded in 1496) became a type of entity that would reappear in every major area of Spanish occupation. The central city formed a stable head-quarters for the Spaniards in the midst of a chaos of population loss and economic shifts in the countryside. On the city's edge were the ranchos, impermanent structures inhabited mainly by Indians temporarily in town for work purposes.

The Spanish Colonization of Mexico

Hernando Cortés set out for the Mexican interior, relying sometimes on force, sometimes on amity toward the local Indian peoples, but always careful to keep conflict with them to a strict minimum.

The leader of the Spain's venture into Mexico in 1519, Hernán (Hernando) Cortés, had some university education and was unusually articulate, but he conformed to the general type of the leader, being senior, wealthy, and powerful, and the expedition he organized was also of the usual type. Passing by the Maya of the Yucatán Peninsula, the Spaniards landed in force on the central coast, almost immediately founding Veracruz, which despite small shifts in location has been the country's main port ever since. The Aztec empire, or Triple Alliance, of the city-states of Tenochtitlán, Texcoco, and Tacuba, centering on Tenochtitlán, dominated central Mexico. The coastal peoples among whom the Spaniards landed, however, had only recently been incorporated in the Aztec tribute system, and they gave no resistance.

Moving inland, the invaders encountered the second power of the region, the Tlaxcalans. Tlaxcala briefly engaged the Spaniards in battle but soon decided to ally with them against their traditional enemy, the Aztec. As the Spaniards moved on toward Tenochtitlán, many of the local subordinate states also came to terms. Even in Tenochtitlán itself fighting did not ensue immediately; the Spaniards as usual seized the the king of Tenochtitlán, Montezuma, and began to exercise authority through him. The expected violence was not long in coming, and fighting broke out in the capital. At this point the most unusual part of the process began, for Tenochtitlán was on an island in the midst of a lake. Here the Spaniards lost much of their usual advantage. They were forced from Tenochtitlán with severe casualties. Although they retained their superiority in the open country, they had to retire to Tlaxcala, accumulate reinforcements, and then come back to Tenochtitlán to carry out a unique full-scale siege, including the use of European-style vessels with cannon on the lake. After four months the Spaniards captured the Aztec capital and reclaimed it as Mexico City.

The key to Hernando Cortés's conquest of Mexico lay in the political crisis within the Aztec empire; the Aztecs were bitterly resented by many of the subject peoples who had to pay tribute to them.

English Settlement:
JAMESTOWN COLONY

The Jamestown colony was a private venture, financed and organized by the Virginia Company of London. King James I granted a charter to a group of investors for the establishment of the company on April 10, 1606. The charter gave the company the right to settle anywhere from roughly present-day North Carolina to New York state. The company's plan was to reward investors by locating gold and silver deposits and by finding a river route to the Pacific Ocean for trade with the Orient.

A contingent of approximately 105 colonists departed England in late December 1606 in three ships—the *Susan Constant*, the *Godspeed*, and the *Discovery*—under the command of Christopher Newport. They reached Chesapeake Bay on April 26, 1607.

The colonists' relations with Chief Powhatan and the Powhatan empire were mixed. The two sides conducted business with each other, the English trading their metal tools and other goods for food supplies. At times the Powhatans showed generosity in providing gifts of food to the colony. On other occasions, encounters between the colonists and the tribes turned violent, and the Powhatans occasionally killed colonists who strayed alone outside the fort.

The Early Hardships of Settlement

When Newport returned to England on June 22, 1607, with the *Susan Constant* and the *Godspeed*—leaving the smaller *Discovery* behind for the colonists—he brought with him a positive report from the council in Jamestown to the Virginia Company. The colony's leaders wrote, and probably believed, that the colony was in good condition and on track for success. But the report proved too optimistic. The colonists had not carried out the work in the springtime needed for the long haul, such as building up the food stores and digging a freshwater well. The first mass casualties of the colony took place in August 1607, when a combination of bad water from the James River (where the colony was located), disease-bearing mosquitoes, and limited food rations created a wave of dysentery and severe fevers.

John Smith's Command

John Smith took John Ratcliffe's place as the commander of the Jamestown colony on September 10, 1608, because of Ratcliffe's mismanagement of the colony. To impose discipline on malingering colonists, Smith announced a new rule: "He that will not worke shall not eate (except by sicknesse he be disabled)." Even so, the colony continued to depend on trade with

the Indians for much of its food supply. During Smith's administration, no settlers died of starvation, and the colony survived the winter with minimal losses. In 1609, Smith stepped down as leader of the colony, having been seriously injured when his gunpowder bag caught fire from mysterious causes. He sailed back to England and left the colony to deal with impending and unprecedented hardships.

John Rolfe

Planter John Rolfe's experiments with tobacco beginning in 1612 quickly transformed the settlement. By replacing native Virginia tobacco with more-palatable plants from the West Indies, he was able to raise a product that could compete with Spanish tobacco in the British market. After Rolfe sent his first barrels to England in 1614, other colonists observed his lucrative results and imitated him. By the end of the decade, the colony had virtually a one-crop economy. Rolfe also married the legendary Pocahontas, which brought ease and relative peace to the escalating tensions between the Powhatan Indians and settlers.

The Starving Time

In the autumn of 1609, after Smith left, Chief Powhatan began a campaign to starve the English out of Virginia. The tribes under his rule stopped bartering for food and carried out attacks on English parties that came in search of trade. Hunting became highly dangerous, as the Powhatan Indians also killed Englishmen they found outside the fort. Long reliant on the Indians, the colony found itself with far too little food for the winter.

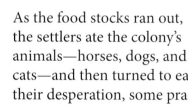

As the food stocks ran out, the settlers ate the colony's animals—horses, dogs, and cats—and then turned to eating rats, mice, and shoe leather. In their desperation, some practiced cannibalism. The winter of 1609–10, commonly known as the Starving Time, took a heavy toll. Of the 500 colonists living in Jamestown in the autumn, fewer than one-fifth were still alive by March 1610. Sixty were still in Jamestown; another 37, more fortunate, had escaped by ship.

Records concerning the lives and status of the first African Americans are very limited. It can be assumed that they were put to work on the tobacco harvest, an arduous undertaking. English law at this time did not recognize hereditary slavery, and it is possible that they were treated at first as indentured servants (obligated to serve for a specified period of time) rather than as slaves. Clear evidence of slavery in English America does not appear until the 1640s.

The Pilgrims & Plymouth Colony

The Pilgrims who founded Plymouth Colony were religious separatists from the Church of England who, in the search for religious toleration, had immigrated first to the Netherlands and then to North America. They sailed in the *Mayflower* from Plymouth, England, and reached Cape Cod in November 1620.

In the first year of settlement, nearly half the Pilgrim settlers died of disease. From that time forward, however, and despite decreasing support from English investors, the health and the economic position of the colonists improved. The Pilgrims soon secured peace treaties with most of the Indians around them, enabling them to devote their time to building a strong, stable economic base rather than diverting their efforts toward costly and time-consuming problems of defending the colony from attack. Although none of their principal economic pursuits—farming, fishing, and trading—promised them lavish wealth, the Pilgrims in America were, after only five years, self-sufficient.

The first settlers, initially referred to as the Old Comers and later as the Forefathers, did not become known as the Pilgrim Fathers until two centuries after their arrival. Although the Pilgrims were always a minority in Plymouth, they nevertheless controlled the entire governmental structure of their colony during the first four decades of settlement.

Chartered by a group of English merchants called the London Adventurers, the *Mayflower* was prevented by rough seas and storms from reaching the territory that had been granted in Virginia (a region then conceived of as much larger than the present-day U.S. state of Virginia, at the time including the *Mayflower*'s original destination in the area of the Hudson River in what is now New York state).

The Mayflower Compact

Rough seas and storms prevented the *Mayflower* from reaching its intended destination in the area of the Hudson River, and the ship was steered instead toward Cape Cod. Because of the change of course, the passengers were no longer within the jurisdiction of the charter granted to them in England by the Virginia Company. Within this legally uncertain situation, friction arose between the Pilgrims and the rest of the travelers, with some of the latter threatening to leave the group and settle on their own.

To quell the conflict and preserve unity, Pilgrim leaders (among them William Bradford and William Brewster) drafted the Mayflower Compact before going ashore. The brief document bound its signers into a body politic for the purpose of forming a government and pledged them to abide by any laws and regulations that would later be established "for the general good of the colony." The compact was signed by nearly all of the *Mayflower's* adult male passengers (41 of a total of 102 passengers) while the ship was anchored at Provincetown harbor. Its authority was immediately exercised when John Carver, who had helped organize the expedition, was chosen as governor of the new colony.

The First Thanksgiving

Americans generally believe that their Thanksgiving is modeled on a 1621 harvest feast shared by the English settlers of Plymouth and the Wampanoag Indians. Plymouth's Thanksgiving began with a few colonists going out "fowling," possibly for turkeys but more probably for the easier prey of geese and ducks, since they "in one day killed as much as . . . served the company almost a week." Next, 90 or so Wampanoag made a surprise appearance at the settlement's gate, doubtlessly unnerving the 50 or so colonists. Nevertheless, over the next few days the two groups socialized without incident. The Wampanoag contributed venison to the feast, which included the fowl and probably fish, eels, shellfish, stews, vegetables, and beer. The men fired guns, ran races, and drank liquor, struggling to speak in broken English and Wampanoag. This was a rather disorderly affair, but it sealed a

treaty between the two groups that lasted until King Philip's War (1675–76), in which hundreds of colonists and thousands of Indians lost their lives.

Thanksgiving Day did not become an official holiday until Northerners dominated the U.S. federal government. While sectional tensions prevailed in the mid-19th century, the editor of the popular magazine *Godey's Lady's Book*, Sarah Josepha Hale, campaigned for a national Thanksgiving Day to promote unity. She finally won the support of President Abraham Lincoln. On October 3, 1863, during the Civil War, Lincoln proclaimed a national day of thanksgiving to be celebrated on Thursday, November 26.

WILLIAM BRADFORD
GOVERNOR AND HISTORIAN
OF THE
PLYMOUTH COLONY

William Bradford

As a boy in England, William Bradford was caught up in the fervor of the Protestant Reformation and when he was only 12 became a dedicated member of one of the separatist churches that made up the "left wing" of Puritanism. Seven years later he joined a group of nonconformists who migrated to Holland (1609) in search of religious freedom. Dissatisfied with the lack of economic opportunity there, he helped organize an expedition of about 100 "Pilgrims" to the New World in 1620. They made up about half the passengers on the *Mayflower*. Aboard ship, Bradford was one of the framers of the historic Mayflower Compact, an agreement for voluntary civil cooperation that became the foundation of the Plymouth government. The following year he was unanimously chosen as governor of the New World settlement and was re-elected 30 times, serving all but five years until 1656.

The Puritans
and Massachusetts Bay Colony

The Puritans of the Massachusetts Bay Colony, like the Pilgrims, sailed to America principally to free themselves from religious restraints. Unlike the Pilgrims, the Puritans did not desire to "separate" themselves from the Church of England but, rather, hoped by their example to reform it. Nonetheless, one of the recurring problems facing the leaders of the Massachusetts Bay colony was to be the tendency of some, in their desire to free themselves from the alleged corruption of the Church of England, to espouse Separatist doctrine. When these tendencies or any other hinting at deviation from orthodox Puritan doctrine developed, those holding them were either quickly corrected or expelled from the colony. The leaders of the Massachusetts Bay enterprise never intended their colony to be an outpost of toleration in the New World; rather, they intended it to be a "Zion in the wilderness," a model of purity and orthodoxy, with all backsliders subject to immediate correction.

Despite the authoritarian tendencies of the Massachusetts Bay colony, a spirit of community developed there as perhaps in no other colony. The same spirit caused the residents of Massachusetts to report on their neighbors for deviation from the true principles of Puritan morality also prompted them to be extraordinarily solicitous about their neighbors' needs.

John Winthrop

During the late 1620s, John Winthrop felt increasingly trapped by the economic slump that reduced his landed income and by England's King Charles I's belligerent anti-Puritan policy, which cost him his court post in 1629. When, in 1629, the Massachusetts Bay Company obtained a royal charter to plant a colony in New England, Winthrop joined the company, pledging to sell his English estate and take his family to Massachusetts if the company government and charter were also transferred to America. The other members agreed to these terms and elected him governor (October 20).

After struggling six weeks with "a feverish distemper," John Winthrop died, age 61, in the spring of 1649. By force of character Winthrop had persuaded the colonists to adopt many—though by no means all—of his pet social and political ideas. The detailed journal that he kept during his years in America is a prime source for the early history of Massachusetts.

For the remaining 19 years of his life, Winthrop lived in the New England wilderness, a father figure among the colonists. In the annual Massachusetts elections he was chosen governor 12 times between 1631 and 1648, and during the intervening years he sat on the court of assistants or colony council. In the early 1630s, he did his most creative work, guiding the colonists as they laid out a network of tightly organized towns, each with its church of self-professed saints. Winthrop himself settled at Boston, which quickly became the capital and chief port of Massachusetts. His new farm on the Mystic River was much inferior to his former estate at Groton, but Winthrop never regretted the move, because he was free at last to build a godly commonwealth.

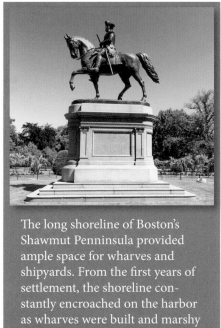

The long shoreline of Boston's Shawmut Penninsula provided ample space for wharves and shipyards. From the first years of settlement, the shoreline constantly encroached on the harbor as wharves were built and marshy coves were filled. West of the original settlement lay Boston Common (pictured here), a tract that has remained public open space since its purchase by the town in 1634.

Theocracy in Massachusetts Bay Colony

The civil government of the colony was guided by an authoritarian spirit. Men such as John Winthrop believed that it was the duty of the governors of society not to act as the direct representatives of their constituents but rather to decide, independently, what measures were in the best interests of the total society. The original charter of 1629 gave all power in the colony to a General Court composed of only a small number of shareholders in the company. On arriving in Massachusetts, many disfranchised settlers immediately protested against this provision and caused the franchise to be widened to include all church members. These "freemen" were given the right to vote in the General Court once each year for a governor and a Council of Assistants. Although the charter of 1629 technically gave the General Court the power to decide on all matters affecting the colony, the members of the ruling elite initially refused to allow the freemen in the General Court to take part in the lawmaking process on the grounds that their numbers would render the court inefficient.

Although life in Massachusetts was made difficult for those who dissented from the prevailing orthodoxy, it was marked by a feeling of attachment and community for those who lived within the enforced consensus of the society. Many New Englanders, however, refused to live within the orthodoxy imposed by the ruling elite of Massachusetts, and both Connecticut and Rhode Island were founded as a by-product of their discontent.

The New England Puritans fashioned the civil commonwealth according to the framework of the church. Only the elect could vote and rule. When this raised problems for second-generation residents, they adopted the Half-Way Covenant, which permitted baptized, moral, and orthodox persons to share the privileges of church membership.

The Colonies

Isolated from the mother country, the colonies evolved representative governments, stressing town meetings, an expanded franchise, and civil liberties. The area was initially distinguished by the self-sufficient farm, but its abundant forests, streams, and harbors soon promoted the growth of a vigorous shipbuilding industry as well as of seaborne commerce across the Atlantic Ocean.

Delaware

The Dutch founded the first European settlement in Delaware at Lewes (then called Zwaanendael) in 1631. They quickly set up a trade in beaver furs with the Native Americans, who within a short time raided and destroyed the settlement after a disagreement between the two groups. A permanent settlement was not established until 1638—by Swedes at Fort Christina (now Wilmington) as part of their colony of New Sweden; they reputedly erected America's first log cabins there.

Pennsylvania

In March 1681 Charles II of England signed a charter giving any unoccupied regions to William Penn in payment of a debt owed by the king to Penn's father. The charter, which was officially proclaimed on April 2, 1681, named the territory for Admiral Penn and included also the term *sylvania* ("woodlands"), at the son's request.

William Penn intended that the colony provide a home for his fellow Quakers (members of the Society of Friends).

New Jersey

Before the Europeans arrived, the Delaware (or Lenni Lenape) Indians had long occupied the region. In 1524 the Italian explorer Giovanni da Verrazzano was the first European to reach New Jersey. Almost a century passed before colonization began with the arrival in 1609 of the English navigator Henry Hudson, who sent a party to explore Sandy Hook Bay. The first permanent European settlement was established by the Dutch at Bergen (now Jersey City) in 1660. The colony was brought under English rule in 1664, although for the next nine years the Dutch disputed that claim.

Connecticut

In contrast to many of the other New England areas, relations between Native Americans and the early settlers in Connecticut were good. Trading posts were established along the Connecticut River by the Dutch from New Amsterdam and by the English from the Plymouth colony, but the first permanent European settlers in the state came from the Massachusetts Bay Colony to the middle Connecticut River valley during 1633–35 and to the Saybrook–New Haven coastal strip during 1635–38.

Maryland

In 1632 Cecilius Calvert was granted a charter for the land around Chesapeake Bay as a haven in which his fellow Roman Catholics might escape the restrictions placed on them in England. The first governor of the proprietary colony, Leonard Calvert, the younger brother of Cecilius, landed the founding expedition on St. Clements Island in the lower Potomac in March 1634. The first settlement and capital was St. Marys City.

Cecilius Calvert

The long-standing dispute between Maryland and Pennsylvania over their common border was settled in 1767 when Great Britain recognized latitude 39°43' N as the legal boundary. The boundary was named the Mason and Dixon Line for its surveyors.

New Hampshire

The New Hampshire region was included in a series of grants made by the English crown to Capt. John Mason and others during the 1620s. A fishing and trading settlement was established in 1623, and in 1629 the name New Hampshire, after the English county of Hampshire, was applied to a grant for a region between the Merrimack and Piscataqua rivers.

New York

New York was originally settled as a colony of the Netherlands following Henry Hudson's exploration in 1609 of the river later named for him. In 1624 at what is today Albany, the Dutch established Fort Orange as the first permanent European settlement in New York. One year later New Amsterdam was established at the southern end of Manhattan Island. To legalize that settlement, Peter Minuit, the Dutch governor, paid the Indians merchandise worth about 60 Dutch guilders at the time—converted to the legendary $24.

Rhode Island

The local people, the Narragansett, welcomed Roger Williams, a refugee from Massachusetts Bay Colony, and sold him the land to found Providence in 1636. Williams, a pioneer of religious liberty, believed in the separation of church and state and had been banished from Massachusetts for his beliefs. His settlement was the first place in America where government ruled "only in civil things," and it attracted other dissenters.

In January 1636, Williams set out for Narragansett Bay, and in the spring, on land purchased from the Narragansett Indians, he founded the town of Providence and the colony of Rhode Island.

The Colonies

The South's warm climate offered 17th- and 18th-century European settlers a superb opportunity to raise crops for export if an adequate permanent labor supply could be found. The source proved to be African slaves, made available for purchase through the international slave trade. From this unique situation of supply and demand arose the system of plantation slavery, which above all other factors distinguished the South from other U.S. regions.

One of the original English colonies and one of the first states in the union, Georgia emerged after the American Revolution as a plantation society that grew rice and cotton and depended heavily on a growing black African slave population.

Georgia

About 1540, Spanish explorer Hernando de Soto, on a quest for silver and gold, led the first European expedition into the area that is now Georgia. There he encountered the highly organized agriculturalists of Mississippian culture. Directly or indirectly, the Spanish expedition was disastrous for the indigenous population. In addition to the hundreds of people they killed or enslaved, the explorers were ultimately responsible—through the diseases they unknowingly introduced, such as measles, smallpox, and whooping cough—for the deaths of thousands and the final decline of the Mississippian culture in Georgia.

The first English settlement in Georgia was made at Savannah in 1733. Some colonists paid their way; the colony's trustees paid the expenses of others.

South Carolina

The first Europeans to visit South Carolina, in 1521, were Spanish explorers from Santo Domingo (Hispaniola). In 1526 Lucas Vásquez de Ayllón founded what is believed to have been the first white European settlement in South Carolina, but this Spanish colony failed within a few months. French Protestants under Jean Ribaut made an unsuccessful attempt to occupy the area of Port Royal (one of the Sea Islands) in 1562.

In 1665 Edward Hyde, 1st earl of Clarendon, and seven other members of the British nobility received a charter from King Charles II to establish the colony of Carolina (named for the king) in a vast territory between latitudes 29° and 36°30' N and from the Atlantic to the Pacific Ocean. These eight grantees were known as the lords proprietor of Carolina, and they were free to dispose of the land as they pleased.

Initially, the English relied for their dependent labor primarily on indentured servants from the mother country. But in the two decades of the 1660s and 1670s the laws of slave ownership were clarified, and the price of servants may have increased because of rising wage rates in prospering England; soon thereafter African slaves replaced English indentured laborers.

In 1585 Sir Walter Raleigh sent a group of settlers to North America, and they established a colony on Roanoke Island; Raleigh named the colony Virginia. Difficulties in obtaining food led many settlers to abandon the island and return to England.

North Carolina

Following the attempts by Raleigh and others to colonize the coastal regions in the 1580s, the territory remained the domain of native peoples for decades. A grant by King Charles I in 1629 for the lands south of Virginia brought the term Carolina into being, but no permanent settlement was made until farmers and traders from Virginia moved into the Albemarle Sound area in the 1650s. This resulted in a grant from England's King Charles II in 1663 that created Carolina, but for years the settlers resisted the ineffective government imposed by the proprietors in England. Between 1712 and 1729 the separate province of North Carolina was ruled by a deputy dispatched from Charleston, which had become the centre of proprietary government. Boundaries between North and South Carolina were agreed upon in 1735 but not completely surveyed until 1821.

The final circum-Caribbean slave society was what became the southern United States. Slaves first were brought to Virginia in 1619. Subsequently, Africans were transshipped to North America from the Caribbean in increasing numbers. Tobacco initially was the profitable crop that occupied most slaves in the Chesapeake.

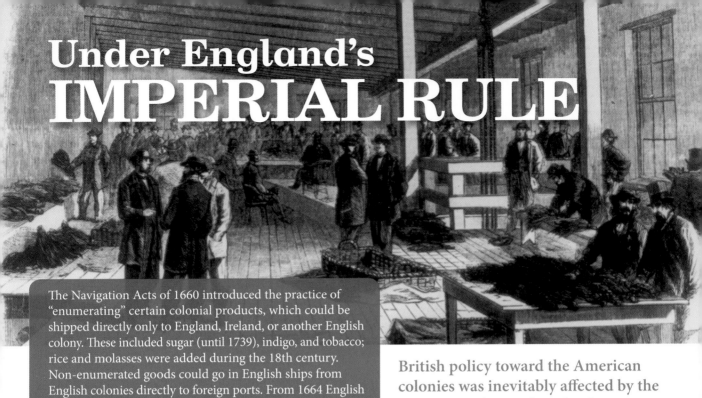

Under England's
IMPERIAL RULE

The Navigation Acts of 1660 introduced the practice of "enumerating" certain colonial products, which could be shipped directly only to England, Ireland, or another English colony. These included sugar (until 1739), indigo, and tobacco; rice and molasses were added during the 18th century. Non-enumerated goods could go in English ships from English colonies directly to foreign ports. From 1664 English colonies could receive European goods only via England.

British policy toward the American colonies was inevitably affected by the domestic politics of England; since the politics of England in the 17th and 18th centuries were never wholly stable, it is not surprising that British colonial policy during those years never developed along clear and consistent lines. During the first half century of colonization, it was even more difficult for England to establish an intelligent colonial policy because of the very disorganization of the colonies themselves. It was nearly impossible for England to predict what role Virginia, Maryland, Massachusetts, Connecticut, and Rhode Island would play in the overall scheme of empire because of the diversity of the aims and governmental structures of those colonies. By 1660, however, England had taken the first steps in reorganizing her empire in a more profitable manner.

Britain's Royal Control

The 1660 act proved inadequate to safeguard the entire British commercial empire, and in subsequent years other navigation acts were passed, strengthening the system. In 1663 Parliament passed an act requiring all vessels with European goods bound for the colonies to pass first through English ports to pay customs duties. In order to prevent merchants from shipping the enumerated articles from colony to colony in the coastal trade and then taking them to a foreign country,

The Navigation Act of 1660 provided that goods bound to England or to English colonies, regardless of origin, had to be shipped only in English vessels; that three-fourths of the personnel of those ships had to be Englishmen; and that certain "enumerated articles," such as sugar, cotton, and tobacco, were to be shipped only to England, with trade in those items with other countries prohibited. This last provision hit Virginia and Maryland particularly hard; although those two colonies were awarded a monopoly over the English tobacco market at the same time that they were prohibited from marketing their tobacco elsewhere.

By the mid-18th century most political power in America was concentrated in the hands of provincial rather than royal officials. These provincial leaders undoubtedly represented the interests of their constituents more faithfully than any royal official could, but it is clear that the politics of provincial America were hardly democratic by modern standards. In general, both social prestige and political power tended to be determined by economic standing, and the economic resources of colonial America, though not as unevenly distributed as in Europe, were nevertheless controlled by relatively few men.

in 1673 Parliament required that merchants post bond guaranteeing that those goods would be taken only to England. Finally, in 1696 Parliament established a Board of Trade to oversee Britain's commercial empire, instituted mechanisms to ensure that the colonial governors aided in the enforcement of trade regulations, and set up vice admiralty courts in America for the prosecution of those who violated the Navigation Acts. On the whole, this attempt at imperial consolidation—what some historians have called the process of Anglicization—was successful in bringing the economic activities of the colonies under closer crown control. While a significant amount of colonial trade continued to evade British regulation, it is nevertheless clear that the British were at least partially successful in imposing greater commercial and political order on the American colonies during the period from the late-17th to the mid-18th century.

In addition to the agencies of royal control in England, there were a number of royal officials in America responsible not only for aiding in the regulation of Britain's commercial empire but also for overseeing the internal affairs of the colonies. The weaknesses of royal authority in the politics of provincial America were striking, however. In some areas, particularly in the corporate colonies of New England during the 17th century and in the proprietary colonies throughout their entire existence, direct royal authority in the person of a governor responsible to the crown was nonexistent. The absence of a royal governor in those colonies had a particularly deleterious effect on the enforcement of trade regulations. In fact, the lack of royal control over the political and commercial activities of New England prompted the Board of Trade to overturn the Massachusetts Bay charter in 1684 and to consolidate Massachusetts, along with the other New England colonies and New York, into the Dominion of New England. After the colonists, aided by the turmoil of the Glorious Revolution of 1688 in England, succeeded in overthrowing the dominion scheme, the crown installed a royal governor in Massachusetts to protect its interests.

The distance separating England and America, the powerful pressures exerted on royal officials by Americans, and the inevitable inefficiency of any large bureaucracy all served to weaken royal power and to strengthen the hold of provincial leaders on the affairs of their respective colonies.

THE FRENCH & INDIAN WAR

French and Indian War was the American phase of a worldwide nine year war (1754–63) fought between France and Great Britain. (The more-complex European phase was the Seven Years' War [1756–63].) It began over the specific issue of whether the upper Ohio River valley was a part of the British Empire, and therefore open for trade and settlement by Virginians and Pennsylvanians, or part of the French Empire. It determined control of the vast colonial territory of North America.

By defeating and securing the French stronghold at Quebec in 1759, the British established a strong presence in New France, foreshadowing the eventual defeat of the French and the beginning of British hegemony in North America. However, the removal of France as a North American power increased the confidence of British colonies such as New York, Pennsylvania, and Massachusetts, which subsequently agitated for greater independence from Great Britain.

Initial Hostilities

A conflict between the two colonial powers over their rival North American claims was doubtless inevitable, but because their areas of trade exploitation were widely separated, that conflict might have been delayed for many years had not the governor-general of New France forced the issue. Although the French had a scant presence in the neighborhood of the Allegheny River and the upper Ohio River where Pennsylvania traders were concentrated, in 1749 the governor-general ordered Pierre-Joseph Céloron de Blainville to compel the trading houses in that region to lower the British flags that flew above them. The traders, regarded as trespassers on French lands, were ordered to retreat to the eastern slopes of the Appalachians. This directive did not have the desired effect, however, and force was applied in 1752 when the important British colonial trading center at Pickawillany on the upper Great Miami River was destroyed. That move was followed by the capture or killing of every English-speaking trader that the French and their Indian allies could find in the upper Ohio Valley. Those actions struck directly not only at the people of Pennsylvania but also at those of Virginia. The government of Virginia took the position that the lands of the upper Ohio were clearly included in the colony's 1609 charter. It argued that this grant gave Virginia a claim to the western lands that was more valid than New France's claim, which was based upon La Salle's much later journey down the Mississippi. In harmony with this point of view, the governor and council of Virginia had by the end of 1752 conditionally granted about 2,300 square miles (6,000 square km) of land in the Ohio Valley to settlers.

PLAN
DU FORT
CARILLON
Echelle

In July 1758 Gen. James Abercrombie attacked the French stronghold at the northern end of Lake George, Fort Carillon (later renamed Fort Ticonderoga).

British Advantages

In reaction to an early string of French victories, in 1757 William Pitt, a formidable British statesman who had been sidelined by his political enemies, assumed control of the British war effort.

In Pitt's favor were factors that were destined to permit him to overwhelm his opponents. One was the growing superiority of the British Royal Navy, which slowly but relentlessly swept French merchantmen, warships, and troop transports from the seas, thus shutting off the means of taking reinforcements of troops and munitions from France to Canada. Moreover, in Great Britain there were vastly greater financial and industrial resources available than there were in France, which was faced with national bankruptcy and economic paralysis before the end of the struggle. The British colonies also had great quantities of food of all sorts for provisioning armies in the field, whereas the inhabitants of French Canada faced almost famine conditions when the blockades off the coast of France and in the Gulf of St. Lawrence made it virtually impossible to import food.

The Treaty of Paris

France, faced with disastrous defeats in the New World, was ready to negotiate a treaty of peace, the signing of which took place in Paris on February 10, 1763. According to its terms, France was to cede Canada to Great Britain and to relinquish all claims to the lands lying east of the Mississippi River, outside the environs of New Orleans. Spain, which had joined the conflict in its waning days and failed spectacularly in an attempt to check British ambitions in the Caribbean, was obliged to give up Florida as a condition for the return of Havana, which had been occupied by the British since August 1762. France ceded Louisiana, including New Orleans, to Spain as compensation.

In 1758, a large British army and fleet under General Jeffrey (later Lord) Amherst and Admiral Edward Boscowen besieged and captured Louisbourg. The British then evacuated the French population, and in 1760 they demolished the fortifications after having used Louisbourg as a base for their conquest of Canada.

THE BOSTON MASSACRE

In 1767, in an attempt to recoup the considerable treasure expended in the defense of its North American colonies during the French and Indian War, the British Parliament enacted strict provisions for the collection of revenue duties in the colonies. Those duties were part of a series of four acts that became known as the Townshend Acts, which also were intended to assert Parliament's authority over the colonies, in marked contrast to the policy of salutary neglect that had been practiced by the British government during the early to mid-18th century. The imposition of those duties—on lead, glass, paper, paint, and tea upon their arrival in colonial ports—met with angry opposition from many colonists in Massachusetts. In addition to organized boycotts of those goods, the colonial response took the form of harassment of British officials and vandalism, culminating in the Boston Massacre on March 5, 1770.

The Massacre

With tensions running high in Boston after the funeral of Christopher Seider, an eleven-year-old boy who was shot and killed by boycott-violating merchant Ebenezer Richardson, brawls broke out between soldiers and rope makers in Boston's South End on March 2 and 3. On March 4 British troops searched the rope works owned by John Gray for a sergeant who was believed to have been murdered. Gray, having heard that British troops were going to attack his workers on Monday, March 5, consulted with Col. William Dalrymple, the commander of the 14th Regiment. Both men agreed to restrain those in their charge, but rumours of an imminent encounter flew.

On the morning of March 5 someone posted a handbill ostensibly from the British soldiers

promising that they were determined to defend themselves. That night a crowd of Bostonians roamed the streets, their anger fueled by rumours that soldiers were preparing to cut down the so-called Liberty Tree, an elm tree in South Boston from which effigies of men who had favored the Stamp Act (a British taxation of all colonial commercial and legal papers, newspapers, pamphlets, cards, almanacs, and dice) had been hung and on the trunk of which was a copper-plated sign that read "The Tree of Liberty," and that a soldier had attacked an oysterman. Emboldened by the knowledge that the Riot Act had not been read—and that the soldiers could not fire their weapons until it had been read and

Widely publicized, the Boston Massacre contributed to the unpopularity of the British regime in much of North America in the years before the American Revolution.

and Thomas Jefferson. John Hancock and John Jay were among those who served as president. The Congress "adopted" the New England military forces that had converged upon Boston and appointed Washington commander in chief of the American army on June 15, 1775. It also acted as the provisional government of the 13 colony-states, issuing and borrowing money, establishing a postal service, and creating a navy. Although the Congress for some months maintained that the Americans were struggling for their rights within the British Empire, it gradually cut tie after tie with Britain until separation was complete. On July 2, 1776, with New York abstaining, the Congress "unanimously" resolved that "these United Colonies are, and of right ought to be, free and independent states." Two days later it solemnly approved this Declaration of Independence. The Congress also prepared the Articles of Confederation, which, after being sanctioned by all the states, became the first U.S. constitution in March 1781.

John Hancock

In 1774 and 1775 Hancock was president of the first and second provincial congresses, and he shared with Samuel Adams the leadership of the Massachusetts Patriots. Hancock was a member of the Massachusetts Constitutional Convention of 1780 and in the same year was elected governor of the state. He served in Congress under the Articles of Confederation in 1785–86 and then returned to the governorship. He presided over the Massachusetts Convention of 1788 that ratified the federal Constitution, although he had been unfriendly at first toward the document. Hancock died while serving his ninth term as governor.

Thomas Jefferson

Jefferson's inveterate shyness prevented him from playing a significant role in the debates within the Second Continental Congress. John Adams, a leader in those debates, remembered that Jefferson was silent even in committee meetings, though consistently staunch in his support for independence. His chief role was as a draftsman of resolutions. In that capacity, on June 11, 1776, he was appointed to a five-person committee, which also included Adams and Benjamin Franklin, to draft a formal statement of the reasons why a break with Great Britain was justified. Adams asked him to prepare the first draft, which he did within a few days. This document is now known as the Declaration of Independence.

Benjamin Franklin

Upon his return to Philadelphia from Britain, where he had been for years working to reconcile the interests of Britain and those of the American colonies, Franklin was immediately elected to the Second Continental Congress, but some Americans remained suspicious of his real loyalties. He had been so long abroad that some thought he might be a British spy. He was delighted that the Congress in 1776 sent him back to Europe as the premier agent in a commission seeking military aid and diplomatic recognition from France. He played on the French aristocracy's liberal sympathies for the oppressed Americans and extracted not only diplomatic recognition of the new republic but also loan after loan from an increasingly impoverished French government.

THE AMERICAN REVOLUTION

The colony of Massachusetts was seen by King George III and his ministers as the hotbed of disloyalty. After the Boston Tea Party (December 16, 1773), Parliament responded with the Intolerable Acts (1774), a series of punitive measures that were intended to cow the restive population into obedience. The 1691 charter of the Massachusetts Bay Colony was abrogated, and the colony's elected ruling council was replaced with a military government under Gen. Thomas Gage, the commander of all British troops in North America. At Gage's headquarters in Boston, he had four regiments— perhaps 4,000 men—under his command, and Parliament deemed that force sufficient to overawe the population in his vicinity. William Legge, 2nd earl of Dartmouth, secretary of state for the colonies, advised Gage that "the violence committed by those, who have taken up arms in Massachusetts, have appeared to me as the acts of a rude rabble, without plan, without concert, without conduct." Gage, for his part, felt that no fewer than 20,000 troops would be adequate for such an endeavor, but he acted with the forces he had at hand.

April 14, 1775, Thomas Gage received a letter from Dartmouth informing him that Massachusetts had been declared to be in a state of open revolt and ordering him to "arrest and imprison the principal Actors and Abettors in the [Massachusetts] Provincial Congress." Gage had received his orders, but the colonials were well aware of his intentions before he could act.

The Battles of Lexington and Concord

Some 700 British troops spent the evening of April 18, 1775, forming ranks on Boston Common, with orders to seize the colonial armory at Concord. The lengthy public display ensured that Gage had lost any chance at secrecy, and by the time the force had been transported across the Charles River to Cambridge it was 2:00 am the following morning. The march to Lexington

was an exercise in misery. It began in a swamp, and the British were forced to wade through brackish water that was, in places, waist deep. By the time the soaked infantrymen arrived in Lexington at approximately 5:00 am, 77 minutemen were among those who had assembled on the village green. Officers on both sides ordered their men to hold their positions but not to fire their weapons. It is unclear who fired "the shot heard 'round the world," but it sparked a skirmish that left eight Americans dead. The colonial force evaporated, and

On April 16, 1775, Paul Revere rode to Concord to urge the patriots to move their military stores, which were endangered by pending British troop movements. At this time he arranged to signal the patriots of the British approach by having lanterns placed in Boston's Old North Church steeple: "One if by land, and two if by sea."

the British moved on to Concord, where they were met with determined resistance from hundreds of militiamen. Now outnumbered and running low on ammunition, the British column was forced to retire to Boston. On the return march, American snipers took a deadly toll on the British, and only the timely arrival of 1,100 reinforcements prevented the retreat from becoming a rout. Those killed and wounded at the Battles of Lexington and Concord numbered 273 British and 95 Americans.

The Battle of Bunker Hill

Rebel militia then converged on Boston from all over New England, while London attempted to formulate a response. Generals Sir William Howe, Sir Henry Clinton, and John Burgoyne were dispatched at once with reinforcements, and Charles Cornwallis followed later. Those four commanders would be identified with the conduct of the principal British operations. The Continental Congress in Philadelphia, acting for the 13 colonies, voted for general defensive measures, called out

Howe's 2,300 troops encountered withering fire while storming the rebel lines at the Battle of Bunker Hill.

troops, and appointed George Washington of Virginia commander in chief. Before Washington could take charge of the 15,000 colonial troops laying siege to the British garrison in Boston, Gage ordered Howe to drive the Americans from the heights in Charlestown, leading to the Battle of Bunker Hill.

The Americans provoked the assault by entrenching on Breed's Hill, the lower of two hills overlooking the British position. The placement of American artillery on the heights would have made the British position in Boston untenable, so on June 17, 1775, Howe led a British frontal assault on the American fortifications. In the misleadingly named Battle of Bunker Hill (Breed's Hill was the primary locus of combat), the British eventually cleared the hill but at the cost of more than 40 percent of the assault force, and the battle was a moral victory for the Americans.

General George Washington

On July 3, 1775, Washington assumed command of the American forces at Cambridge. Not only did he have to contain the British in Boston, but he also had to recruit a Continental army. During the winter of 1775–76 recruitment lagged so badly that fresh drafts of militia were called up to help maintain the siege.

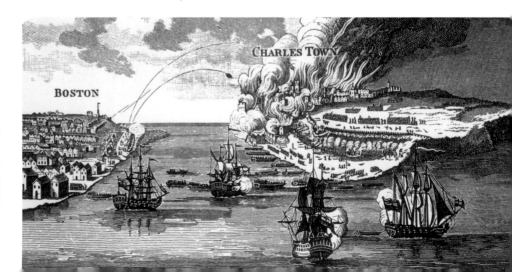

THE AMERICAN REVOLUTION

The Surrender at Saratoga

Britain's strategy in 1777 aimed at driving a wedge between New England and the other colonies. An army under Gen. John Burgoyne was to march south from Canada and join forces with Howe on the Hudson. But Howe seems to have concluded that Burgoyne was strong enough to operate on his own and left New York in the summer, taking his army by sea to the head of Chesapeake Bay. Once ashore, he defeated Washington badly but not decisively at Brandywine Creek on September 11. Then, feinting westward, he entered Philadelphia, the American capital, on September 25. The Continental Congress fled to York. Washington struck back at Germantown on October 4 but, compelled to withdraw, went into winter quarters at Valley Forge.

The most significant result of Burgoyne's capitulation was the entrance of France into the war. The French had secretly furnished financial and material aid since 1776. Now they prepared fleets and armies, although they did not formally declare war until June 1778.

In the North the story was different. Burgoyne was to move south to Albany with a force of about 9,000 British, Germans, Indians, and American loyalists; a smaller force under Lieut. Col. Barry St. Leger was to converge on Albany through the Mohawk valley. Burgoyne took Ticonderoga handily on July 5 and then, instead of using Lake George, chose a southward route by land. Slowed by the rugged terrain, strewn with trees cut down by American axmen under Gen. Philip Schuyler, and needing horses, Burgoyne sent a force of Germans to collect them at Bennington, Vermont. The Germans were nearly wiped out on August 16 by New Englanders under Gen. John Stark and Col. Seth Warner. Meanwhile, St. Leger besieged Fort Schuyler (present-day Rome, New York), ambushed a relief column of American militia at Oriskany on August 6, but retreated as his Indians gave up the siege and an American force approached. Burgoyne himself reached the Hudson, but the Americans, now under Gen. Horatio Gates, checked him at Freeman's Farm on September 19 and, thanks to Arnold's battlefield leadership, decisively defeated him at Bemis Heights on October 7. Ten days later, unable to get help from New York, Burgoyne surrendered at Saratoga.

The French Intervention

The entrance of France into the war, followed by that of Spain in 1779 and the Netherlands in 1780, effected important changes in the naval aspect of the war. The Spanish and Dutch were not particularly active, but their role in keeping British naval forces tied down in Europe was significant. The British navy could not maintain an effective blockade of both the American coast and the enemies' ports. Because of years of neglect, Britain's ships of the line were neither modern nor sufficiently numerous. An immediate result was that France's Toulon fleet under comte d'Estaing got safely away to America, where it appeared off New York and later assisted Maj. Gen. John Sullivan to seige against the British at Newport, Rhode Island. A fierce battle off Ushant, France, in July 1778 between the Channel fleet under Adm. Augustus Keppel and the Brest fleet under the comte d'Orvilliers proved inconclusive. Had Keppel won decisively, French aid to the Americans would have diminished.

Some scholars claim that the British counted too strongly on loyalist support they did not receive.

Cornwallis surrendered his army of more than 7,000 men on October 19, 1781. Thereafter, land action in America died out, though the war persisted in other theaters and on the high seas. While the peace treaties were under consideration and afterward, the British evacuated thousands of loyalists from America, including many from Savannah on July 11, 1782, and others from Charleston on December 14. The last British forces finally left New York on November 25, 1783. Washington then reentered the city in triumph.

Aftermath

Preliminary articles of peace were signed on November 30, 1782, and the Peace of Paris (September 3, 1783) ended the U.S. War of Independence. Great Britain recognized the independence of the United States (with western boundaries to the Mississippi River)

Washington, a rock in adversity, learned slowly but reasonably well the art of generalship.

and ceded Florida to Spain. Other provisions called for payment of U.S. private debts to British citizens, American use of the Newfoundland fisheries, and fair treatment for American colonials loyal to Britain.

In explaining the outcome of the war, scholars have pointed out that the British never contrived an overall general strategy for winning it. Also, even if the war could have been terminated by British power in the early stages, the generals during that period, notably Howe, declined to make a prompt, vigorous, intelligent application of that power. They acted, to be sure, within the conventions of their age, but in choosing to take minimal risks, they lost the opportunity to deal potentially mortal blows to the rebellion.

The Declaration of
INDEPENDENCE

On April 19, 1775, when armed conflict began between Britain and the 13 colonies (the nucleus of the future United States), the Americans claimed that they sought only their rights within the British Empire. At that time few of the colonists consciously desired to separate from Britain. As the American Revolution proceeded during 1775–76 and Britain undertook to assert its sovereignty by means of large armed forces, making only a gesture toward conciliation, the majority of Americans increasingly came to believe that they must secure their rights outside the empire. The losses and restrictions that came from the war greatly widened the breach between the colonies and the mother country; moreover, it was necessary to assert independence in order to secure as much French aid as possible.

On April 12, 1776, the revolutionary convention of North Carolina specifically authorized its delegates in Congress to vote for independence. On May 15 the Virginia convention instructed its deputies to offer the motion, which was brought forward in the Congress by Richard Henry Lee on June 7. By that time the Congress had already taken long steps toward severing ties with Britain. It had denied Parliamentary sovereignty over the colonies as early as December 6, 1775, and it had declared on May 10, 1776, that the authority of the king ought to be "totally suppressed," advising all the several colonies to establish governments of their own choice.

The Declaration of Independence was written largely by Jefferson, who had displayed talent as a political philosopher and polemicist in his *A Summary View of the Rights of British America*, published in 1774.

The Nature and Influence of the Declaration of Independence

It can be said, as John Adams did, that the declaration contained nothing really novel in its political philosophy, which was derived from John Locke, Algernon Sidney, and other English theorists. It may also be asserted that the argument offered was not without flaws in history and logic. Substantially abandoning contention on the basis of the rights of Englishmen, the declaration put forth the more fundamental doctrines of natural rights and of government under social contract. Claiming that Parliament never truly possessed sovereignty over the colonies and that the crown of right exercised it only under contract, the declaration contended that George III, with the support of a "pretended" legislature, had persistently violated the agreement between himself as governor and the Americans as the governed. A long list of accusations was offered toward proving this contention. The right and duty of revolution were then invoked.

The Declaration of Independence has been a source of inspiration outside the United States. It encouraged Antonio de Nariño and Francisco de Miranda to strive toward overthrowing the Spanish empire in South America, and it was quoted with enthusiasm by the Marquis de Mirabeau during the French Revolution.

The Sole Author?

On July 3–4 the Congress debated and edited Jefferson's draft, deleting and revising fully one-fifth of the text. At the time, Jefferson himself was disconsolate that the Congress had seen fit to make any changes in his language. Nevertheless, he was not regarded by his contemporaries as the author of the Declaration, which was seen as a collective effort by the entire Congress. Indeed, he was not known by most Americans as the principal author until the 1790s.

Social-Contract Theory and John Locke

A social contract, in political philosophy, is an actual or hypothetical compact, or agreement, between the ruled and their rulers, defining the rights and duties of each. In primeval times, according to the theory, individuals were born into an anarchic state of nature, which was happy or unhappy according to the particular version. They then, by exercising natural reason, formed a society (and a government) by means of a contract among themselves.

Theories of the social contract differed according to their purpose: some were designed to justify the power of the sovereign; on the other hand, some were intended to safeguard the individual from oppression by an all-too-powerful sovereign.

John Locke (in the second of *Two Treatises of Government*, 1690) described the state of nature as one in which the rights of life and property were generally recognized under natural law, the inconveniences of the situation arising from insecurity in the enforcement of those rights. He therefore argued that the obligation to obey civil government under the social contract was conditional upon the protection not only of the person but also of private property. If a sovereign violated these terms, he could be justifiably overthrown.

The Articles of Confederation

The Articles of Confederation, the first U.S. constitution (1781–89), served as a bridge between the initial government by the Continental Congress of the Revolutionary period and the federal government provided under the U.S. Constitution of 1787. Because the experience of overbearing British central authority was vivid in colonial minds, the drafters of the Articles deliberately established a confederation of sovereign states. The Articles were written in 1776–77 and adopted by the Congress on November 15, 1777. However, the document was not fully ratified by the states until March 1, 1781.

On paper, the Congress had power to regulate foreign affairs, war, and the postal service and to appoint military officers, control Indian affairs, borrow money, determine the value of coin, and issue bills of credit. In reality, however, the Articles gave the Congress no power to enforce its requests to the states for money or troops, and by the end of 1786 governmental effectiveness had broken down.

U.S. Continental Congress, 1777

ARTICLES
OF
CONFEDERATION
AND
PERPETUAL UNION
BETWEEN THE
STATES
OF
NEW-HAMPSHIRE, MASSACHUSETTS-BAY, RHODE-ISLAND AND PROVIDENCE PLANTATIONS, CONNECTICUT, NEW-YORK, NEW-JERSEY, PENNSYLVANIA, DELAWARE, MARYLAND, VIRGINIA, NORTH CAROLINA, SOUTH CAROLINA AND GEORGIA.

WILLIAMSBURG:
Printed by J. DIXON & W. HUNTER.
M,DCC,LXXVIII.

The Confederation provided the new nation with instructive experience in self-government under a written document. In revealing their own weaknesses, the Articles paved the way for the Constitutional Convention of 1787 and the present form of U.S. government.

The framers of the Constitution were especially concerned with limiting the power of government and securing the liberty of citizens. The doctrine of legislative, executive, and judicial separation of powers, the checks and balances of each branch against the others, and the explicit guarantees of individual liberty were all designed to strike a balance between authority and liberty—the central purpose of American constitutional law.

Among the powers delegated to Congress are the right to levy taxes, borrow money, regulate interstate commerce, provide for military forces, declare war, and determine member seating and rules of procedure. The House initiates impeachment proceedings, and the Senate adjudicates them.

The Constitution of the United States of America

The Constitution was written during the summer of 1787 in Philadelphia, Pennsylvania, by 55 delegates to a Constitutional Convention that was called ostensibly to amend the Articles of Confederation (1781–89). The Constitution was the product of political compromise after long and often rancorous debates over issues such as states' rights, representation, and slavery. Delegates from small and large states disagreed over whether the number of representatives in the new federal legislature should be the same for each state—as was the case under the Articles of Confederation—or different depending on a state's population. In addition, some delegates from Northern states sought to abolish slavery or, failing that, to make representation dependent on the size of a state's free population. At the same time, some Southern delegates threatened to abandon the convention if their demands to keep slavery and the slave trade legal and to count slaves for representation purposes were not met. Eventually the framers resolved their disputes by adopting a proposal put forward by the Connecticut delegation.

The Great Compromise, as it came to be known, created a bicameral legislature with a Senate, in which all states would be equally represented, and a House of Representatives, in which representation would be apportioned on the basis of a state's free population plus three-fifths of its slave population. (The inclusion of the slave population was known separately as the three-fifths compromise.) In June 1788, after the Constitution had been ratified by nine states (as required by Article VII), Congress set March 4, 1789, as the date for the new government to commence proceedings (the first elections under the Constitution were held late in 1788). Because ratification in many states was contingent on the promised addition of a Bill of Rights, Congress proposed 12 amendments in September 1789; 10 were ratified by the states, and their adoption was certified on December 15, 1791. (One of the original 12 proposed amendments, which prohibited midterm changes in compensation for members of Congress, was ratified in 1992 as the Twenty-seventh Amendment. The last one, concerning the ratio of citizens per member of the House of Representatives, has never been adopted.)

Washington arrived in Philadelphia on May 13, 1787, the day before the opening of the Constitutional Convention, and as soon as a quorum was obtained he was unanimously chosen its president. For four months he presided over the convention, breaking his silence only once upon a minor question of congressional apportionment. Although he said little in debate, no one did more outside the hall to insist on stern measures. "My wish is," he wrote, "that the convention may adopt no temporizing expedients, but probe the defects of the Constitution to the bottom, and provide a radical cure."

THE BILL OF RIGHTS

The Bill of Rights derives from the Magna Carta (1215), the English Bill of Rights (1689), the colonial struggle against king and Parliament, and a gradually broadening concept of equality among the American people. Virginia's 1776 Declaration of Rights, drafted chiefly by George Mason, was a notable forerunner. Besides being axioms of government, the guarantees in the Bill of Rights have binding legal force. Acts of Congress in conflict with them may be voided by the U.S. Supreme Court when the question of the constitutionality of such acts arises in litigation.

Popular dissatisfaction with the limited guarantees of the main body of the Constitution expressed in the state conventions called to ratify it, led to demands and promises that the first Congress of the United States satisfied by submitting to the states 12 amendments. Ten were ratified. Individual states being subject to their own bills of rights, these amendments were limited to restraining the federal government. The Senate refused to submit James Madison's amendment (approved by the House of Representatives) protecting religious liberty, freedom of the press, and trial by jury against violation by the states.

Elected to the new House of Representatives, James Madison sponsored the first 10 amendments to the Constitution—the Bill of Rights—placing emphasis in debate on freedom of religion, speech, and press. His leadership in the House, which caused the Massachusetts congressman Fisher Ames to call him "our first man," came to an end when he split with Secretary of the Treasury Alexander Hamilton over methods of funding the war debts. Hamilton's aim was to strengthen the national government by cementing men of wealth to it; Madison sought to protect the interests of Revolutionary veterans.

Our Bill of Rights

TRIAL BY JURY

IS EVERYBODY'S BUSINESS

"**We the People of the United States,** in Order to form a more perfect Union, establish Justice, insure domestic Tranquility, provide for the common defense, promote the general Welfare, and secure the Blessings of Liberty to ourselves and our Posterity, do ordain and establish this Constitution for the United States of America."

–Preamble to the Constitution of the United State of America

The Amendments

Under the First Amendment, Congress can make no law respecting an establishment of religion or prohibiting its free exercise, or abridging freedom of speech or press or the right to assemble and petition for redress of grievances. Hostility to standing armies found expression in a guarantee of the people's right to bear arms and in limitation of the quartering of soldiers in private houses.

The Second Amendment reads, "A well regulated Militia, being necessary to the security of a free State, the right of the people to keep and bear Arms, shall not be infringed." In addition to checking federal power, the Second Amendment also provided state governments with what Luther Martin (1744/48–1826) described as the "last coup de grace" that would enable the states "to thwart and oppose the general government." Last, it enshrined the ancient Florentine and Roman constitutional principle of civil and military virtue by making every citizen a soldier and every soldier a citizen. The Third Amendment prohibits the involuntary quartering of soldiers in private homes. Although the Third Amendment has never been the direct subject of Supreme Court scrutiny, its core principles were among the most salient at the time of the founding of the republic.

The Fourth Amendment secures the people against unreasonable searches and seizures and forbids the issuance of warrants except upon probable cause and directed to specific persons and places. The Fifth Amendment requires grand jury indictment in prosecutions for major crimes and prohibits double jeopardy for a single offense. It provides that no person shall be compelled to testify against himself, forbids the taking of life, liberty, or property without due process of law or the taking of private property for public use without just compensation.

By the Sixth Amendment, an accused person is to have a speedy public trial by jury, to be informed of the nature of the accusation, to be confronted with prosecution witnesses, and to have the assistance of counsel. The Seventh Amendment's objective was to preserve a distinction between the responsibilities of the courts (such as deciding matters of law) and those of juries (such as deciding matters of fact).

Excessive bail or fines and cruel or unusual punishment are forbidden by the Eighth Amendment.

The Ninth Amendment protects unenumerated residual rights of the people, and by the Tenth, powers not delegated to the United States are reserved to the states or the people.

The United States Capitol is the meeting place of the United States Congress and one of the most familiar landmarks in Washington, D.C. The Supreme Court held sessions in the Capitol until its own building was completed in 1935.

The Founding of the Capital in
WASHINGTON D.C.

Washington was established as the capital of the United States as the result of a compromise following seven years of negotiation by members of the U.S. Congress as they tried to define the concept of a "federal enclave." On July 17, 1790, Congress passed the Residence Act, which created a permanent seat for the federal government. George Washington, the country's first president (1789–97), carefully chose the site, which is on the Potomac River's navigation head (to accommodate oceangoing ships), and near two well-established colonial port cities, George Town (now Georgetown, a section of the city of Washington) and Alexandria, Va. This location bridged the Northern and Southern states, but Washington called it "the gateway to the interior" because he hoped it would also serve to economically bind the Western territories to the Eastern Seaboard—the Tidewater and the Piedmont regions—and thereby secure the allegiance of the frontier to the new country.

The new federal territory was named District of Columbia to honor explorer Christopher Columbus, and the new federal city was named for George Washington. In 1790 French-born American engineer and designer Pierre-Charles L'Enfant was chosen to plan the

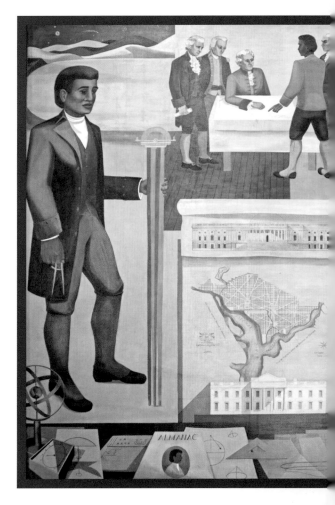

new capital city; meanwhile, surveyor Andrew Ellicott surveyed the 10-square-mile (26-square-km) territory with the assistance of Benjamin Banneker, a self-educated free black man. The territory surveyed by Ellicott was ceded by Virginia, a Southern state with the largest slave population, thus contributing to a significant black presence in Washington.

Construction of the Capitol building, the presidential palace (now the White House), and several other government buildings was almost complete when Congress moved from Philadelphia to Washington in December 1800. There were, however, few finished dwellings and even fewer amenities in Washington at the time, making the first several years rather unpleasant for the new residents. In 1812 the United States declared war against Great Britain, and two years later the British invaded the vulnerable capital city, setting fire to federal buildings. Structural damage was extensive, and the morale of the local citizens sank.

Design and Construction

Pierre Charles L'Enfant, who had designed the basic plan of Washington, was also expected to design the Capitol. Claiming that the plan was "in his head," however, L'Enfant refused to submit drawings or work with local commissioners, and President George Washington was forced to dismiss him. A plan by William Thornton, a versatile physician with no formal architectural training, was eventually accepted, though it was submitted months after the closure of a design competition held in 1792.

Because Thornton had no knowledge of building technology, the construction was initially supervised by the runner-up in the competition, Stephen Hallet. Hallet attempted to alter many of Thornton's plans and was quickly replaced, first by George Hadfield and later by James Hoban, the architect who designed the White House.

William Thornton

In 1788, William Thornton became a U.S. citizen and settled in Philadelphia. Without any formal study of architecture, Thornton in 1789 won a building design competition promoted by the Library Company of Philadelphia. From 1790 to 1792 he was in the British Virgin Islands, where he first heard of the important competition for the Capitol at Washington. He submitted designs that were received months after the competition closed; yet the judges, not satisfied with those previously submitted, selected Thornton's. His revised Georgian design of 1795 was executed as the exterior of the north and south wings adjacent to the central rotunda, though Benjamin H. Latrobe completely redesigned the interiors.

An image of the inauguration of Abraham Lincoln in 1861. At the insistence of President Abraham Lincoln, work on the dome continued during the Civil War as an important symbol of national unity.

William Thornton's 1793 sketch of the United States Capitol. Thomas Jefferson, who was then secretary of state, was impressed with Thornton's design, writing that it "so captivated the eyes and judgment of all as to leave no doubt...of its preference over all which have been produced....It is simple, noble, beautiful, excellently distributed and moderate in size."

Benjamin Banneker

Banneker, a freeman, was raised on a farm near Baltimore that he would eventually inherit from his father. Although he periodically attended a one-room Quaker schoolhouse, Banneker was largely self-educated and did much of his learning through the voracious reading of borrowed books. As early as 1788, Banneker began to make astronomical calculations, and he accurately predicted a solar eclipse that occurred in 1789. In 1791, while working with Andrew Ellicott and others in surveying the land that would become Washington, D.C., Banneker made other astronomical observations. As an essayist and pamphleteer, Banneker opposed slavery and advocated civil rights. In 1791 he sent Thomas Jefferson, then U.S. secretary of state, a letter asking Jefferson's aid in bringing about better conditions for African Americans.

U.S. Expansion: THE LOUISIANA PURCHASE

The first serious disruption of French control over Louisiana came during the Seven Years' War. In 1762 France ceded Louisiana west of the Mississippi River to Spain and in 1763 transferred virtually all of its remaining possessions in North America to Great Britain. This arrangement, however, proved temporary. French power rebounded under the subsequent military leadership of Napoleon Bonaparte, and on October 1, 1800, Napoleon induced a reluctant King Charles IV of Spain to agree, for a consideration, to cede Louisiana back to France. King Charles gave at least his verbal assent on the condition that France would never alienate the territory to a third power. With this treaty of retrocession, known as the Treaty of San Ildefonso (confirmed March 21, 1801), would go not only the growing and commercially significant port of New Orleans but the strategic mouth of the Mississippi River.

In 1800 the Spanish returned Louisiana to France, and three years later the United States, under the leadership of Pres. Thomas Jefferson, bought Louisiana from the French emperor Napoleon I. The Louisiana Purchase, a vast acquisition of land for the country, included New Orleans and much of present-day Louisiana state, as well as most of the territory between the Mississippi River and the Rocky Mountains.

Reports of the supposed retrocession soon were received by the U.S. government with deep misgivings. During the preceding 12 years, Americans had streamed westward into the valleys of the Cumberland, Tennessee, and Ohio rivers. The very existence of these new settlers depended on their right to use the Mississippi River freely and to make transshipment of their exports at New Orleans. By terms of the Treaty of San Lorenzo, Spain, in 1795, had granted to the United States the right to ship goods originating in American ports through the mouth of the Mississippi without paying duty and also the right of deposit, or temporary storage, of American goods at New Orleans for transshipment. But in 1802 Spain in effect revoked the right of deposit, and so it was in an atmosphere of growing tension in the West that Pres. Thomas Jefferson was confronted with the prospect of a new, wily, and more powerful keeper of the strategic window to the Gulf of Mexico.

Negotiations Between France and the United States

Jefferson instructed Robert R. Livingston, the U.S. minister at Paris, to take two steps: (1) to approach Napoleon's minister, Charles Maurice de Talleyrand, with the object of preventing the retrocession in the event this act had not yet been completed; and (2) to try to purchase at least New Orleans if the property had actually been transferred from Spain to France. Direct negotiations with Talleyrand, however, appeared to be all but impossible. Livingston had but one trump to play, and he played it with a flourish. He made it known that a rapprochement with Great Britain might, after all, best serve the interests of his country, and at that particular moment an Anglo-American rapprochement was about the least of Napoleon's desires.

There are good reasons to believe that French failure in Santo Domingo, the imminence of renewed war with Great Britain, and financial stringencies may all have prompted Napoleon in 1803 to offer for sale to the United States the entire Louisiana Territory.

Defining the Purchase

JEFFERSON

A treaty was signed on May 2 but was antedated to April 30. By its terms the Louisiana Territory, in the form France had received it from Spain, was sold to the United States. For this vast domain the United States agreed to pay $11,250,000 outright and assumed claims of its citizens against France in the amount of $3,750,000. Interest payments incidental to the final settlement made the total price $27,267,622.

Much of the territory turned out to contain rich mineral resources, productive soil, valuable grazing land, forests, and wildlife resources of inestimable value. Out of this empire were carved in their entirety the states of Louisiana, Missouri, Arkansas, Iowa, North Dakota, South Dakota, Nebraska, and Oklahoma; in addition, the area included most of the land in Kansas, Colorado, Wyoming, Montana, and Minnesota.

The major achievement of Thomas Jefferson's first term was also an act of defiance, though this time it involved defying his own principles. In 1803 Napoleon decided to consolidate his resources for a new round of the conflict with England by selling the vast Louisiana region. Even before news that the purchase was approved reached the United States in July 1803, Jefferson dispatched his private secretary, Meriwether Lewis, to lead an expedition to explore the new acquisition and the lands beyond, all the way to the Pacific.

Precisely what the United States had purchased was unclear. The wording of the treaty was vague; it did not clearly describe the boundaries. It gave no assurances that West Florida was to be considered a part of Louisiana; neither did it delineate the southwest boundary. The American negotiators were fully aware of this.

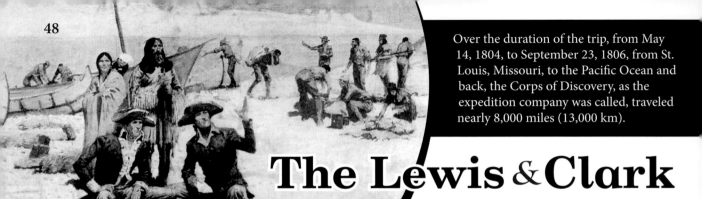

Over the duration of the trip, from May 14, 1804, to September 23, 1806, from St. Louis, Missouri, to the Pacific Ocean and back, the Corps of Discovery, as the expedition company was called, traveled nearly 8,000 miles (13,000 km).

The Lewis & Clark EXPEDITION

On January 18, 1803, U.S. Pres. Thomas Jefferson sent a secret message to Congress asking for $2,500 to send an officer and a dozen soldiers to explore the Missouri River, make diplomatic contact with Indians, expand the American fur trade, and locate the Northwest Passage (the much-sought-after hypothetical northwestern water route to the Pacific Ocean). Jefferson, who had already sponsored several attempts to explore the West, asked his personal secretary, Meriwether Lewis, to lead the expedition. Lewis was dispatched to Philadelphia for instruction in botany, celestial navigation, medicine, and zoology. He also purchased supplies and spent $20 on a Newfoundland dog, Seaman.

As his co-commander he selected William Clark, who had been his military superior during the government's battles with the Northwest Indian Federation in the early 1790s. The U.S. secretary of war denied Lewis's request of a shared command, but Captain Lewis and Lieutenant Clark chose to address one another as "captain" to hide this fact from the other members of the expedition.

The expedition encountered immense animal herds and ate well, consuming one buffalo, two elk, or four deer per day, supplemented by roots, berries, and fish. They named geographic locations after expedition members, peers, loved ones, and even their dog (Seaman's Creek). They experienced dysentery, venereal disease, boils, tick bites, and injuries from prickly pear, yet only one man perished over the course of the journey.

Expedition From May 14, 1804, to October 16, 1805

The entourage, numbering about four dozen men, covered 10 to 20 miles (16 to 32 km) a day—poling, pushing, and pulling their 10-ton keelboat and two pirogues (dugout boats) up the Missouri River. Lewis's iron-framed boat was later assembled and covered with skins near Great Falls (in present-day Montana) but had to be abandoned because the seams leaked and there was no pitch to seal them. The captains and at least five others kept journals.

Wintering in what is now North Dakota , the captains prepared maps, artifacts, mineral samples, plant specimens, and papers to send back in the spring. On April 7, 1805, a small crew departed on a St. Louis-bound keelboat laden with boxes of materials for Jefferson that included live magpies and a prairie dog. Meanwhile, the permanent party proceeded up the Missouri in six canoes and two pirogues. It now consisted of 33 people, including soldiers, civilians, Clark's slave York, and two newly hired interpreters—a French Canadian, Toussaint Charbonneau, and his Shoshone wife, Sacagawea, who had given birth to a boy, Jean Baptiste, that February.

Arriving at the Three Forks of the Missouri River (the confluence of the Jefferson, Madison, and Gallatin rivers), Sacagawea recognized Beaverhead Rock and informed the others they would soon encounter some Shoshones. Lewis was dismayed when his hope for a single mountain portage was dashed by the view of the endless Rocky Mountains before him. Fortunately while crossing the Rockies, in mid-August, they met a Shoshone band led by Sacagawea's brother Cameahwait, who provided the expedition with horses. The Shoshone guide Old Toby joined

the expedition and led them across the Bitterroot Range. Cold and hungry, the expedition finally spilled out of the mountains onto the Weippe Prairie, homeland of the Nez Percé. Upon the recommendation of a respected elderly woman, Watkuweis, the Nez Percé befriended the expedition. After leaving their horses with Chief Twisted Hair, the explorers hollowed out five cottonwood canoes and floated down the Clearwater and Snake rivers, reaching the Columbia River on October 16.

Upon climbing the Lemhi Pass in the Bitterroot Range, Lewis recorded, "I discovered immence ranges of high mountains still to the West of us with their tops partially covered with snow." On the crossing, Clark lamented, "I have been wet and as cold in every part as I ever was in my life, indeed I was at one time fearfull my feet would freeze in the thin mockersons [moccasins] which I wore."

The Pacific Ocean and Their Return

They finally arrived at the Pacific Ocean in mid-November, with Clark recording in his journal, "Ocian in view! O! the joy." Fierce storms delayed their progress for nearly a month. The members conducted a democratic vote on where to spend the winter, with even York and Sacagawea casting votes. Near present-day Astoria, Oregon, the corps built Fort Clatsop and endured a wet, miserable winter by journal writing, drying meat, making salt, and traveling to see a beached whale. They hoped to encounter vessels along the Pacific that could transport them home, but, finding none, they did an about-face, planning to return along the Columbia and Missouri rivers. After stealing a Clatsop Indian canoe, they headed up the Columbia on March 23, 1806. They arrived at the Nez Percé villages, gathered up their horses, and waited for the snows to melt.

The Corps of Discovery met with a grand reception at St. Louis on September 23. Congress rewarded them with double pay and public land. The captains each received 1,600 acres (650 hectares), and their men received 320 acres (130 hectares). The final cost for the expedition totaled $38,000. Jefferson appointed Lewis governor of Upper Louisiana Territory and appointed Clark an Indian agent.

The War of 1812

Neither the British in Canada nor the United States were prepared for war.

After Jefferson became president in 1801, relations with Britain slowly deteriorated. Compounding this situation, the British decision to blockade French ports prompted the French emperor, Napoleon, to cut off Britain from European and American trade. The Berlin Decree (November 21, 1806) established Napoleon's Continental System, which impinged on U.S. neutral rights by designating ships that visited British ports as enemy vessels. The British responded with Orders in Council (November 11, 1807) that required neutral ships to obtain licenses at English ports before trading with France or French colonies. In turn, France announced the Milan Decree (December 17, 1807), which strengthened the Berlin Decree by authorizing the capture of any neutral vessel that had submitted to search by the British. Consequently, American ships that obeyed Britain faced capture by the French in European ports, and if they complied with Napoleon's Continental System, they could fall prey to the Royal Navy.

Under increasing pressure, Pres. James Madison, who had taken office in 1809, summoned the U.S. Congress into session in November 1811. Pro-war western and southern Republicans (War Hawks) assumed a vocal role, especially after Kentucky War Hawk Henry Clay was elected speaker of the House of Representatives. Madison sent a war message to the U.S. Congress on June 1, 1812, and signed the declaration of war on June 18, 1812. The vote seriously divided the House (79–49) and was gravely close in the Senate (19–13). Because seafaring New Englanders opposed the war, while westerners and southerners supported it, Federalists accused war advocates of expansionism under the ruse of protecting American maritime rights. Expansionism, however, was not as much a motive as was the desire to defend American honor. The United States attacked Canada because it was British, but no widespread aspiration existed to incorporate the region. The prospect of taking East and West Florida from Spain encouraged southern support for the war, but southerners, like westerners, were sensitive about the United States's reputation in the world. Furthermore, British commercial restrictions hurt American farmers by barring their produce from Europe. Regions seemingly removed from maritime concerns held a material interest in protecting neutral shipping. "Free trade and sailors' rights" was not an empty phrase for those Americans.

The onset of war both surprised and chagrined the British government, especially because it was preoccupied with the fight against France. In addition, political changes in Britain had already moved the government to assume a conciliatory posture toward the United States. Prime Minister Spencer Perceval's assassination on May 11, 1812, brought to power a more moderate Tory government under Lord Liverpool. British West Indies planters had been complaining for years about the interdiction of U.S. trade, and their growing influence, along with a deepening recession in Great Britain, convinced the Liverpool ministry that the Orders in Council were averse to British interests. On June 16, two days before the United States declared war, the Orders were suspended.

Early in the war, the small U.S. navy boosted sagging American morale as officers such as Isaac Hull, Stephen Decatur, and William Bainbridge commanded heavy frigates in impressive single-ship actions. The British Admiralty responded by instructing captains to avoid individual contests with Americans, and within a year the Royal Navy had blockaded important American ports, bottling up U.S. frigates. British Adm. George Cockburn also conducted raids on the shores of Chesapeake Bay. In 1814, Britain extended its blockade from New England to Georgia, and forces under John Sherbrooke occupied parts of Maine.

British raids in Chesapeake Bay directed by Adm. Alexander Cochrane were successful compared to other raids. British Gen. Robert Ross captured Washington (August 24, 1814) and burned government buildings, including the United States Capitol and the Executive Mansion (now known as the White House). The British justified this action as retaliation for the American destruction of York (modern Toronto), the capital of Upper Canada, the previous year.

Fort McHenry
The British assault on Baltimore (September 12–14, 1814) foundered when Americans fended off an attack at Northpoint and withstood the naval bombardment of Fort McHenry, an action that inspired Francis Scott Key's "Star-Spangled Banner."

The Aftermath

Contention in the United States had hobbled the war effort, and domestic disaffection had menaced the Union, but after the war a surge of patriotism inspired Americans to pursue national goals. Contrary to American expectations, Canada remained British and eventually developed its own national identity, partly from pride over repulsing U.S. invasions. Meanwhile, Britain's influence among the northwestern Indians was forever ended, and American expansion in that region proceeded unchecked. In the South, the Creek War opened a large part of that region for settlement and led to the events that persuaded Spain to cede Florida to the United States in 1821. The war was ended by the Treaty of Ghent in December 1814, although the news did not reach the troops in time to prevent a final British defeat by Gen. Andrew Jackson's forces in Jauary 1815.

SLAVERY

Captured Africans were generally marched in chains to the coast and crowded into the holds of slave ships for the dreaded Middle Passage across the Atlantic Ocean, usually to the West Indies.

The uninterrupted history of blacks in the United States began in 1619, when 20 Africans were landed in the English colony of Virginia. These individuals were not slaves but indentured servants—persons bound to an employer for a limited number of years—as were many of the settlers of European descent (whites). By the 1660s large numbers of Africans were being brought to the English colonies. In 1790 blacks numbered almost 760,000 and made up nearly one-fifth of the population of the United States.

Attempts to hold black servants beyond the normal term of indenture culminated in the legal establishment of black chattel slavery in Virginia in 1661 and in all the English colonies by 1750. Black people were easily distinguished by their skin color (the result of evolutionary pressures favoring the presence in the skin of a dark pigment called melanin in populations in equatorial climates) from the rest of the populace, making them highly visible targets for enslavement. Moreover, the development of the belief that they were an "inferior" race with a "heathen" culture made it easier for whites to rationalize black slavery. Enslaved blacks were put to work clearing and cultivating the farmlands of the New World.

Of an estimated 10 million Africans brought to the Americas by the slave trade, about 430,000 came to the territory of what is now the United States. The overwhelming majority were taken from the area of western Africa stretching from present-day Senegal to Angola, where political and social organization as well as art, music, and dance were highly advanced. On or near the African coast had emerged the major kingdoms of Oyo, Ashanti, Benin, Dahomey, and the Congo. In the Sudanese interior had arisen the empires of Ghana, Mali, and Songhai; the Hausa states; and the states of Kanem-Bornu. Such African cities as Djenné and Timbuktu, both now in Mali, were at one time major commercial and educational centres.

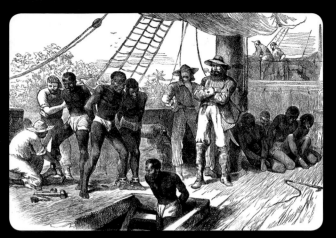

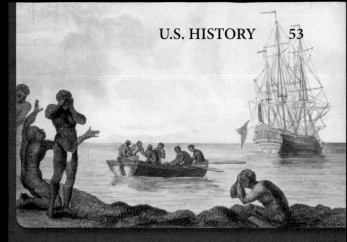

Once a ship was loaded, the trip know as "the Middle Passage," usually to Brazil or an island in the Caribbean, was a matter of a few weeks to several months. Between 1500 and the end of the 19th century the time of voyage diminished considerably. That change was important, because death rates, which ranged from around 10 to more than 20 percent on the Middle Passage, was directly proportional to the length of the voyage.

The Middle Passage

The Middle Passage was the forced voyage of enslaved Africans across the Atlantic Ocean to the New World. It was one leg of the triangular trade route that took goods from Europe to Africa, Africans to work as slaves in the Americas and West Indies, and items, mostly raw materials, produced on the plantations back to Europe. Slaver captains anchored chiefly off the Guinea Coast (also called the Slave Coast) for a month to a year to trade for their cargoes of 150 to 600 persons, most of whom had been kidnapped and forced to march to the coast under wretched conditions. While at anchor and after the departure from Africa, those aboard ship were exposed to almost continuous dangers, including raids at port by hostile tribes, epidemics, attack by pirates or enemy ships, and bad weather. Despite—or perhaps in part because of—the conditions aboard ship, some Africans who survived the initial horrors of captivity revolted; male slaves were kept constantly shackled to each other or to the deck to prevent mutiny, of which 55 detailed accounts were recorded between 1699 and 1845.

Black slaves played a major, though unwilling and generally unrewarded, role in laying the economic foundations of the United States—especially in the South. Blacks also played a leading role in the development of Southern speech, folklore, music, dancing, and food, blending the cultural traits of their African homelands with those of Europe.

Laws known as the slave codes regulated the slave system to promote absolute control by the master and complete submission by the slave. Under these laws the slave was chattel—a piece of property and a source of labor that could be bought and sold like an animal. The slave was allowed no stable family life and little privacy. Slaves were prohibited by law from learning to read or write. The meek slave

received tokens of favor from the master, and the rebellious slave provoked brutal punishment. A social hierarchy among the plantation slaves also helped keep them divided. At the top were the house slaves; next in rank were the skilled artisans; at the bottom were the vast majority of field hands, who bore the brunt of the harsh plantation life.

SLAVERY
in the United States of America

During the 17th and 18th centuries, African and African American (those born in the New World) slaves worked mainly on the tobacco, rice, and indigo plantations of the Southern seaboard. Eventually slavery became rooted in the South's huge cotton and sugar plantations. Although Northern businessmen made great fortunes from the slave trade and from investments in Southern plantations, slavery was never widespread in the North.

Historians concur that the emphasis on the slave as property was a requisite for dehumanizing the Africans. Says the historian Philip D. Morgan, "The only effective way to justify slavery was to exclude its victims from the community of man."

Crispus Attucks, a former slave killed in the Boston Massacre of 1770, was the first martyr to the cause of American independence from Great Britain. During the American Revolution, some 5,000 black soldiers and sailors fought on the American side. After the Revolution, some slaves—particularly former soldiers—were freed, and the Northern states abolished slavery. But with the ratification of the Constitution of the United States, in 1788, slavery became more firmly entrenched than ever in the South. The Constitution counted a slave as three-fifths of a person for purposes of taxation and representation in Congress (thus increasing the number of representatives from slave states), prohibited Congress from abolishing the African slave trade before 1808, and provided for the return of fugitive slaves to their owners.

In 1807 Pres. Thomas Jefferson signed legislation that officially ended the African slave trade beginning in January 1808. However, this act did not presage the end of slavery. Rather, it spurred the growth of the domestic slave trade in the United States, especially as a source of labor for the new cotton lands in the Southern interior. Increasingly, the supply of slaves came to be supplemented by the practice of "slave breeding," in which women slaves were persuaded to conceive as early as age 13 and to give birth as often as possible.

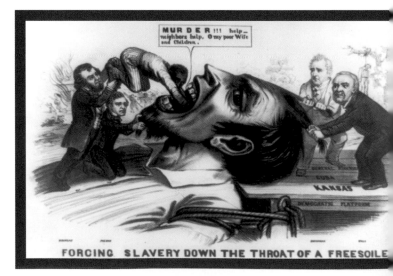

FORCING SLAVERY DOWN THE THROAT OF A FREESOILE

Free Blacks and Abolitionism

During the period of slavery, free blacks made up about one-tenth of the entire African American population. In 1860 there were almost 500,000 free African Americans —half in the South and half in the North. The free black population originated with former indentured servants and their descendants. It was augmented by free black immigrants from the West Indies and by blacks freed by individual slave owners.

The earliest African American leaders emerged among the free blacks of the North, particularly those of Philadelphia, Boston, and New York City. Free African Americans in the North established their own institutions—churches, schools, and mutual aid societies. One of the first of these organizations was the African Methodist Episcopal (AME) church, formed in 1816 and led by Bishop Richard Allen of Philadelphia. Among other noted free African Americans was the astronomer and mathematician Benjamin Banneker.

The American antislavery movement, linked to the "Second Great Awakening," succeeded in arousing immense hostility between the non-slave North, where most states had voluntarily abolished slavery by 1804, and the slaveholding South, where the "peculiar institution" became even further entrenched because of the spread of cotton cultivation.

Free blacks were among the first abolitionists. They included John B. Russwurm and Samuel E. Cornish, who in 1827 founded *Freedom's Journal*, the first African American-run newspaper in the United States. Black support also permitted the founding and survival of the *Liberator*, a journal begun in 1831 by the white abolitionist William Lloyd Garrison. Probably the most celebrated of all African American journals was the *North Star*, founded in 1847 by the former slave Frederick Douglass, who argued that the antislavery movement must be led by black people.

Many learned people on both sides of the Atlantic disputed the moral rightness of slavery. Opponents argued that a society of free men working for wages would be better producers of goods and services. But pro-slavery forces, which included some of the wealthiest men in America and England, soon posed what they came to believe was an unassailable argument for keeping blacks enslaved: the idea of black inferiority.

The Great Chain of Being

A number of 18th-century political and intellectual leaders began publicly to assert that Africans were naturally inferior and that they were indeed best suited for slavery. A few intellectuals revived an older image of all living things, the *scala naturae* (Latin: "scale of nature"), or Great Chain of Being, to demonstrate that nature or God had made men unequal. This ancient hierarchical paradigm—encompassing all living creatures, starting with the simplest organisms and reaching to humans, angels, and ultimately to God—became for the advocates of slavery a perfect reflection of the realities of inequality that they had created. The physical differences of blacks and Indians became the symbols or markers of their status. It was during these times that the term *race* became widely used to denote the ranking and inequality of these peoples—in other words, their placement on the Chain of Being.

The Missouri Compromise

The territory of Missouri first applied for statehood in 1817, and by early 1819 Congress was considering enabling legislation that would authorize Missouri to frame a state constitution. When Rep. James Tallmadge of New York attempted to add an antislavery amendment to that legislation on February 13, 1819, however, there ensued an ugly and rancorous debate over slavery and the government's right to restrict slavery. The Tallmadge amendment prohibited the further introduction of slaves into Missouri and provided for emancipation of those already there when they reached age 25. The amendment passed the House of Representatives, controlled by the more-populous North, but failed in the Senate, which was equally divided between free and slave states. Congress adjourned without resolving the Missouri question.

When it reconvened in December 1819, Congress was faced with a request for statehood from Maine. The Senate passed a bill allowing Maine to enter the Union as a free state and Missouri to be admitted without restrictions on slavery. Sen. Jesse B. Thomas of Illinois then added an amendment that allowed Missouri to become a slave state but banned slavery in the rest of the Louisiana Purchase north of latitude 36°30'. Henry Clay then skillfully led the forces of compromise, engineering separate votes on the controversial measures. On March 3, 1820, the decisive votes in the House admitted Maine as a free state, Missouri as a slave state, and made free soil all western territories north of Missouri's southern border.

Dred Scott did, in fact, get his freedom, but not through the courts. After he and his wife were later bought by the Blow family (who had sold Scott to Emerson in the first place), they were freed in 1857.

Supreme Court Chief Justice Roger B. Taney is remembered now almost solely for the blatantly pro-slavery decision he wrote and for his demeaning comments about African Americans. When he died in 1864, he was roundly denounced and vilified in the North.

Sectional conflict would grow to the point of civil war after the Missouri Compromise was repealed by the Kansas-Nebraska Act (1854) and was declared unconstitutional in the Dred Scott decision of 1857.

The Dred Scott Decision

Dred Scott was a slave who was owned by John Emerson of Missouri. In 1834 Emerson undertook a series of moves as part of his service in the U.S. military. He took Scott from Missouri (a slave state) to Illinois (a free state) and finally into the Wisconsin Territory (a free territory). During this period, Scott met and married Harriet Robinson, who became part of the Emerson household. Emerson married in 1838, and in the early 1840s he and his wife returned with the Scotts to Missouri, where Emerson died in 1843. Dred Scott reportedly attempted to purchase his freedom from Emerson's widow, who refused the sale. In 1846, with the help of antislavery lawyers, Harriet and Dred Scott filed individual lawsuits for their freedom in Missouri state court in Saint Louis on the grounds that their residence in a free state and a free territory had freed them from the bonds of slavery.

The Dred Scott decision, formally the *Dred Scott v. John F.A. Sandford*, was a legal case in which the U.S. Supreme Court on March 6, 1857, ruled (7–2) that Dred Scott who had resided in a free state and territory (where slavery was prohibited) was not thereby entitled to his freedom; that African Americans were not and could never be citizens of the United States; and that the Missouri Compromise (1820), which had declared free all territories west of Missouri and north of latitude 36°30', was unconstitutional. The decision added fuel to the sectional controversy and pushed the country closer to civil war. Among constitutional scholars, *Scott v. Sandford* is widely considered the worst decision ever rendered by the Supreme Court.

The Monroe Doctrine

The Monroe Doctrine (December 2, 1823) was the cornerstone of U.S. foreign policy enunciated by Pres. James Monroe in his annual message to Congress. Declaring that the Old World and New World had different systems and must remain distinct spheres, Monroe made four basic points: (1) the United States would not interfere in the internal affairs of or the wars between European powers; (2) the United States recognized and would not interfere with existing colonies and dependencies in the Western Hemisphere; (3) the Western Hemisphere was closed to future colonization; and (4) any attempt by a European power to oppress or control any nation in the Western Hemisphere would be viewed as a hostile act against the United States.

The Monroe Doctrine, in asserting unilateral U.S. protection over the entire Western Hemisphere, was a foreign policy that could not have been sustained militarily in 1823.

The Doctrine's Purpose

The first draft of the message included a reproof of the French for their invasion of Spain, an acknowledgement of Greek independence in the revolt against Turkey, and some further indications of American concern in European affairs. Secretary of State John Quincy Adams argued for the better part of two days against such expressions, which were finally eliminated from the message.

Adams noted in his diary, "The ground that I wish to take is that of earnest remonstrance against the interference of the European powers by force in South America, but to disclaim all interference on our part with Europe; to make an American cause, and adhere inflexibly to that." Monroe and Adams were well aware of the need for the British fleet to deter potential aggressors in Latin America. Because the United States was not a major power at the time and because the continental powers apparently had no serious intentions of recolonizing Latin America, Monroe's policy statement (it was not known as the "Monroe Doctrine" for nearly 30 years) was largely ignored outside the United States.

The United States did not invoke the Monroe Doctrine nor oppose British occupation of the Falkland Islands in 1833 or subsequent British encroachments in Latin America. In 1845 and again in 1848, however, Pres. James K. Polk reiterated Monroe's principles in warning Britain and Spain not to establish footholds in Oregon, California, or Mexico's Yucatán Peninsula.

At the conclusion of the American Civil War, the United States massed troops on the Rio Grande in support of a demand that France withdraw its puppet kingdom from Mexico. In 1867—partly because of U.S. pressure—France withdrew.

Later Interpretations

After 1870 interpretation of the Monroe Doctrine became increasingly broad. As the United States emerged as a world power, the Monroe Doctrine came to define a recognized sphere of influence. Pres. Theodore Roosevelt added the Roosevelt Corollary to the Monroe Doctrine in 1904, which stated that, in cases of flagrant and chronic wrongdoing by a Latin American country, the United States could intervene in that country's internal affairs.

From the presidency of Theodore Roosevelt to that of Franklin Roosevelt, the United States frequently intervened in Latin America, especially in the Caribbean. Since the 1930s the United States has attempted to formulate its Latin American foreign policy in consultation with the individual nations of the hemisphere and with the Organization of American States. Yet the United States continues to exercise a proprietary role at times of apparent threat to its national security, and the Western Hemisphere remains a predominantly U.S. sphere of influence.

Roosevelt's assertion of hemispheric police power was designed to preclude violation of the Monroe Doctrine by European countries seeking redress of grievances against unruly or mismanaged Latin American states.

James Monroe

The chief events of Monroe's calm and prosperous administration, which has been called the Era of Good Feelings, were the First Seminole War (1817–18); the acquisition of the Floridas from Spain (1819–21); the Missouri Compromise (1820); recognition of the new Latin American states; and the enunciation, in the presidential message of December 2, 1823, of the Monroe Doctrine, which has profoundly influenced the foreign policy of the United States.

It is generally concluded that Secretary of State John Quincy Adams was the sole author of the noncolonization principle of the doctrine; the principle of abstention from European wars and politics was common to all the fathers of American independence, inherited and expressed by the younger Adams all his professional life; in cabinet meetings, Adams also urged the dictum of nonintervention in the affairs of the nations of the Western Hemisphere. But Adams had no idea of proclaiming these dicta to the world. Monroe took responsibility for embodying them in a presidential message that he drafted himself. Modern historical judgment considers the Monroe Doctrine to be appropriately named.

The Indian Removal Act

The Indian Removal Act of 1830 enabled the president to designate tracts of land west of the Mississippi as new Indian Territories, to negotiate with tribes to effect their removal from east of the Mississippi, and to fund these transactions and associated transportation costs. The Native American population had not been consulted in these matters and responded in a variety of ways. Perhaps the most determined to remain in place were the Seminoles, who fiercely defended their homes; the Seminole Wars came to be the most expensive military actions undertaken by the U.S. government up to that point.

During the first 300 years of colonization, the Southeastern peoples had adopted what new practices they found useful without completely altering their traditional cultures. This was a very successful strategy, and they often became the owners of large, prosperous farms and plantations. As the pressure to cede land to settlers increased, the tribes opted to negotiate with the nascent United States in the belief that treaties and other agreements would be enforced by this government, as they had by Spain, England, and France.

Leading up to the Indian Removal Act

The first full declaration of U.S. policy toward the country's indigenous peoples was embodied in the third of the Northwest Ordinances (1787): "The utmost good faith shall always be observed toward the Indians, their lands and property shall never be taken from them without their consent; and in their property, rights, and liberty, they shall never be invaded or disturbed, unless in just and lawful wars authorized by Congress; but laws founded in justice and humanity shall from time to time be made, for preventing wrongs being done to them, and for preserving peace and friendship with them."

Within a few decades this guarantee of legal, political, and property rights was undermined by a series of Supreme Court decisions and the passage of the Indian Removal Act.

The act was initiated after the 1828 discovery of gold on Cherokee land in Georgia. Speculators hoping to profit from the discovery, including President Andrew Jackson, subsequently pressured Congress to find a way to legally divest the tribe of its land. Jackson's speech *On Indian Removal*, presented to Congress in December 1830, provides a sample, although certainly not a full account, of his rationalizations for such action.

Removal of Southern Tribes

The Cherokees preferred to use legal strategies to maintain their property and the political independence guaranteed to them by treaty. Sequoyah's 1821 invention of a syllable-based writing system for the Cherokee language enabled the wide circulation of a draft Cherokee constitution; tribal members voted to adopt the new constitution in 1827. At the same time, settler agitation regarding the primacy of state versus tribal sovereignty was accelerated by the discovery of gold within the Cherokee Nation lands, and the Georgia legislature in turn passed a law extending state authority to tribal lands; many Euro-Americans felt that tribes should not be allowed to maintain separate governments within state boundaries. Instead, they proposed that tribal members choose between regular citizenship or tribal sovereignty; Indians could either give up the protections provided by treaty agreements or remove themselves to territories outside the states. The Cherokees saw this as a vacuous argument, as their sovereign status was very clearly delineated in the treaties they had negotiated with the federal government. They chose to file suit against the state in federal court.

While the Cherokee lawsuit moved through the judicial system, the United States Congress passed the Indian Removal Act (1830). This enabled the government to designate Indian Territory land in the trans-Mississippi West; it created a process through which land in the new territory would be exchanged for tribal land in the East and provided funds for the transportation of tribes to the new domain.

The Seminoles were a multiethnic group that included Creek and other native refugees who had fled the mid-18th century conflicts, as well as Africans and African Americans who had escaped slavery. A few Seminole leaders signed an agreement of removal in 1832, but the majority of tribal members declared that the agreement was not binding and refused to go; this provoked the Second Seminole War (1835–42), a conflict that the Seminoles eventually lost, with many being forcibly removed to the west.

The Removal Act was enforced throughout the Eastern Woodlands, and very few native individuals remained there after 1840 with some notable exceptions, including groups in Florida, Louisiana, Alabama, and North and South Carolina.

THE TRAIL OF TEARS

Traditionally, the Northeast Indian nations tended to be more mobile and less politically unified than those of the Southeast. As a result, literally dozens of band-specific removal agreements were negotiated with the peoples of that region between 1830 and 1840. Many of the groups residing in the coniferous forests of the Upper Midwest, such as various bands of Ojibwa and Ho-Chunk, agreed to cede particular tracts of land but retained in perpetuity the right to hunt, fish, and gather wild plants and timber from such properties.

In 1829 a gold rush occurred on Cherokee land in Georgia. Vast amounts of wealth were at stake: at their peak, Georgia mines produced approximately 300 ounces of gold a day. Land speculators soon demanded that the U.S. Congress devolve to the states the control of all real property owned by tribes and their members. That position was supported by Pres. Andrew Jackson, who was himself an avid speculator. Congress complied by passing the Indian Removal Act. The act entitled the president to negotiate with the eastern nations to effect their removal to tracts of land west of the Mississippi and provided some $500,000 for transportation and for compensation to native landowners. Jackson reiterated his support for the act in various messages to Congress, notably *On Indian Removal* (1830) and *A Permanent Habitation for the American Indians* (1835), which illuminated his political justifications for removal and described some of the outcomes he expected would derive from the relocation process.

Negotiations and Reactions

Indigenous reactions to the Indian Removal Act varied. The Choctaw were the first polity to finalize negotiations: in 1830 they agreed to cede their real property for western land, transportation for themselves and their goods, and logistical support during and after the journey. However, the federal government had no experience in transporting large numbers of civilians, let alone their household effects, farming equipment, and livestock. Bureaucratic ineptitude and corruption caused many Choctaw to die from exposure, malnutrition, exhaustion, and disease while traveling.

The Chickasaw signed an initial removal agreement as early as 1830, but negotiations were not finalized until 1832.

Groups living in the prairies and deciduous forests of the Lower Midwest, including bands of Sauk, Fox, Iowa, Illinois, and Potawatomi, ceded their land with great reluctance and were moved west in small parties, usually under pressure from speculators, settlers, and the U.S. military.

A few groups attempted armed resistance, most notably a band led by the Sauk leader Black Hawk in 1832. Although their experiences are often overshadowed by those of the more-populous Southeast nations, the peoples of the Northeast constituted perhaps one-third to one-half of those who were subject to removal.

Skeptical of federal assurances regarding reimbursement for their property, members of the Chickasaw nation sold their landholdings at a profit and financed their own transportation. As a result, their journey, which took place in 1837, had fewer problems than did those of the other Southeast tribes.

The Creek also finalized a removal agreement in 1832. However, Euro-American settlers and speculators moved into the planned Creek cessions prematurely, causing conflicts, delays, and fraudulent land sales that delayed the Creek journey until 1836. Federal authorities once again proved incompetent and corrupt, and many Creek people died, often from the same preventable causes that had killed Choctaw travelers.

Traditionally, the Northeast Indian nations tended to be more mobile and less politically unified than those of the Southeast. Many of the groups residing in the coniferous forests of the Upper Midwest, such as various bands of Ojibwa and Ho-Chunk, agreed to cede particular tracts of land but retained in perpetuity the right to hunt, fish, and gather wild plants and timber from such properties.

Cherokee Devastation

The Cherokee chose to use legal action to resist removal. Their lawsuits, notably *Cherokee Nation v. Georgia* (1831) and *Worcester v. Georgia* (1832), reached the U.S. Supreme Court but ultimately provided no relief. As with the Seminole, a few Cherokee leaders negotiated a removal agreement that was subsequently rejected by the people as a whole. Although several families moved west in the mid-1830s, most believed that their property rights would ultimately be respected. This was not to be the case, and in 1838 the U.S. military began to force Cherokee people from their homes, often at gunpoint. Held in miserable internment camps for days or weeks before their journeys began, many became ill, and most were very poorly equipped for the arduous trip. Those who took the river route were loaded onto boats in which they traveled parts of the Tennessee, Ohio, Mississippi, and Arkansas rivers, eventually arriving at Fort Gibson in Indian Territory. Not until then did the survivors receive much-needed food and supplies. Perhaps 4,000 of the estimated 15,000 Cherokee died on the journey, while some 1,000 avoided internment and built communities in North Carolina.

Estimates based on tribal and military records suggest that approximately 100,000 indigenous people were forced from their homes during the 1830s, which is sometimes known as the removal era, and that some 15,000 died during the journey west.

MANIFEST DESTINY

John L. O'Sullivan, the editor of a magazine that served as an organ for the Democratic Party and of a partisan newspaper, first wrote of "manifest destiny" in 1845, but at the time he did not think the words profound. Rather than being "coined," the phrase was buried halfway through the third paragraph of a long essay in the July–August issue of *The United States Magazine, and Democratic Review* on the necessity of annexing Texas and the inevitability of American expansion. O'Sullivan was protesting European meddling in American affairs, especially by France and England, which he said were acting "for the avowed object of thwarting our policy and hampering our power, limiting our greatness and checking the fulfillment of our manifest destiny to overspread the continent allotted by Providence for the free development of our yearly multiplying millions."

O'Sullivan's observation was a complaint rather than a call for aggression, and he referred to demography rather than pugnacity as the solution to the perceived problem of European interference.

Democrats took up Manifest Destiny as a slogan. The phrase frequently appeared in debates relating to Oregon, sometimes as soaring rhetoric and other times as sarcastic derision. As an example of the latter, on February 6, 1846, the *New-Hampshire Statesman and State Journal*, a Whig newspaper, described "some windy orator in the House [of Representatives]" as "pouring for his 'manifest destiny' harangue."

When O'Sullivan expanded his idea on December 27, 1845, in a newspaper column in the *New York Morning News*, the wider audience seized upon his reference to divine superintendence. Discussing the dispute with Great Britain over the Oregon Country, O'Sullivan again cited the claim to "the right of our manifest destiny to overspread and to possess the whole of the continent which Providence has given us for the development of the great experiment of liberty and federated self-government entrusted to us."

A History of Expansion

Despite disagreements about Manifest Destiny's validity at the time, O'Sullivan had stumbled on a broadly held national sentiment. Although it became a rallying cry as well as a rationale for the foreign policy that reached its culmination in 1845–46, the attitude behind Manifest Destiny had long been a part of the American experience. The impatient English who colonized North America in the 1600s and 1700s immediately gazed westward and instantly considered ways to venture into the wilderness and tame it. The cause of that ceaseless wanderlust varied from region to region, but the behavior became a tradition within one generation. The western horizon would always beckon, and Americans would always follow.

After the American Revolution (1775–83), the steady advance of the cotton kingdom in the South matched the lure of the Ohio Country in the North. In 1803, Pres. Thomas Jefferson's Louisiana Purchase doubled the size of the country with the stroke of a pen. Expansionists eager to acquire Spanish Florida were part of the drive for the War of 1812, and many historians argue that American desires to annex Canada were also an important part of the equation. The most consequential territorial expansion in the country's history occurred during the 1820s. Spreading American settlements often caused additional unrest on the country's western borders. As the United States pacified and stabilized volatile regions, the resulting appropriation of territory usually worsened relations with neighbors, setting off a cycle of instability that encouraged additional annexations.

Although the doctrine enabled the U.S. to extend its sovereignty across the continent to the Pacific, to the 49th parallel on the Canadian border, and to the Rio Grande in the south, not all Americans found expansion encouraging. Those dissenters saw rapid expansion as contrary to the principles of a true republic and predicted that the cost of empire would be high and its consequences perilous.

Before the American Civil War (1861–65), the idea of Manifest Destiny was used to validate continental acquisitions in the Oregon Country, Texas, New Mexico, and California. The purchase of Alaska after the Civil War briefly revived the concept of Manifest Destiny, but it most evidently became a renewed force in U.S. foreign policy in the 1890s, when the country went to war with Spain, annexed Hawaii, and laid plans for an isthmian canal across Central America.

The End of Manifest Destiny

Realizing its Manifest Destiny with triumph over Mexico in 1848 gave the United States an immense domain that came with spectacular abundance and potential. (Under the Treaty of Guadalupe Hidalgo, which ended the Mexican-American War, the United States acquired more than 525,000 square miles of land, including present-day Arizona, California, western Colorado, Nevada, New Mexico, Texas, and Utah.) California's climate made much of it a natural garden, and its gold would finance decades of impressive growth. Burgeoning Pacific trade required opening diplomatic relations with heretofore isolationist Japan and created American trade in places that before had always been European commercial preserves. Yet the dispute over the status of the new western territories regarding slavery disrupted the American political system by reviving arguments that shattered fragile compromises and inflamed sectional discord. In fact, those disputes brought the era of Manifest Destiny to an abrupt close.

The Mexican-American War

BATTLE OF BUENA VISTA.

When war broke out, former Mexican president and general Antonio López de Santa Anna (the vanquisher of the Texan forces at the Alamo in 1836) contacted Polk. The U.S. president arranged for a ship to take Santa Anna from his exile in Cuba to Mexico for the purpose of working for peace. Instead of acting for peace, however, on his return, Santa Anna took charge of the Mexican forces.

The tensions that led to the Mexican-American War (April 1846–February 1848) began when Mexico severed relations with the U.S. in March 1845. James K. Polk sent diplomat and former congressman John Slidell on a secret mission to Mexico City to negotiate the disputed Texas border, settle U.S. claims against Mexico, and purchase New Mexico and California for up to $30 million. Mexican Pres. José Joaquín Herrera, aware in advance of Slidell's intention of dismembering the country, refused to receive him. When Polk learned of the snub, he ordered troops under Gen. Zachary Taylor to occupy the disputed area between the Nueces and the Rio Grande (January 1846).

On May 9, Polk began to prepare a war message to Congress, justifying hostilities on the grounds of Mexican refusal to pay U.S. claims and refusal to negotiate with Slidell. That evening he received word that Mexican troops had crossed the Rio Grande on April 25 and attacked Taylor's troops, killing or injuring 16 of them. In his quickly revised war message—delivered to Congress on May 11—Polk claimed that Mexico had "invaded our territory and shed American blood on American soil."

Congress overwhelmingly approved a declaration of war on May 13, but the United States entered the war divided. Democrats, especially those in the Southwest, strongly favored the conflict. Most Whigs viewed Polk's motives as conscienceless land grabbing. In December 1846 Polk accused his Whig doubters of treason. In January 1847 the by-then Whig-controlled House voted 85 to 81 to censure Polk for having "unnecessarily and unconstitutionally" initiated war with Mexico.

Invasion and War

Following its original plan for the war, the United States sent its army from the Rio Grande, under Taylor, to invade the heart of Mexico while a second force, under Col. Stephen Kearny, was to occupy New Mexico and California. Kearny's campaign into New Mexico and California encountered little resistance, and the residents of both provinces appeared to accept U.S. occupation with a minimum of resentment. Meanwhile, Taylor's army fought several battles south of the Rio Grande, captured the important city of Monterrey, and defeated a major Mexican force at the Battle of Buena Vista in February 1847.

But Taylor showed no enthusiasm for a major invasion of Mexico, and on several occasions he failed to pursue the Mexicans vigorously after defeating them. In disgust, Polk revised his war strategy. He ordered Gen. Winfield Scott to take an army by sea to Veracruz, capture that key seaport, and march inland to Mexico City. Despite some Mexican resistance, Scott's campaign was marked by an unbroken series of victories, and he entered Mexico City on September 14, 1847. The fall of the Mexican capital ended the military phase of the conflict. Ultimately, infection and disease took many more U.S. casualties than combat did. At least 10,000 troops died of illness, whereas some 1,500 were killed in action or died of battle wounds (estimates of the war's casualties vary).

The Battle of Palo Alto (May 8,1846) was the first clash in the Mexican War, fought at a small site in southeastern Texas. General Taylor and his army met the invaders at Palo Alto with superior artillery. Despite the greater numbers and crack cavalry units of the Mexican army, commanded by General Mariano Arista, the Mexicans suffered heavier casualties. Disheartened by their lack of success, they retired the next day to a defensive position farther south.

Chapultepec was the scene of the last-ditch Mexican resistance in the war between Mexico and the United States. U.S. forces under General Winfield Scott, having seized Veracruz on the Gulf of Mexico, and then advanced on the capital. In his path was the hill of Chapultepec, with approximately 5,000 defenders, including cadets from Mexico's military academy. After heavy artillery bombardment on September 12, 1847, failed to force their withdrawal, Scott's forces attacked the next morning. The defenders resisted in fierce hand-to-hand combat before capitulating.

Treaty of Guadalupe Hidalgo and the War's Legacy

Polk had assigned Nicholas Trist, chief clerk in the State Department, to accompany Scott's forces and to negotiate a peace treaty. But after a long delay in the formation of a new Mexican government capable of negotiations, Polk grew impatient and recalled Trist. Trist, however, disobeyed his instructions and on February 2, 1848, signed the Treaty of Guadalupe Hidalgo. According to the treaty, which was subsequently ratified by both national congresses, Mexico ceded to the United States nearly all the territory now included in the states of New Mexico, Utah, Nevada, Arizona, California, Texas, and western Colorado for $15 million and U.S. assumption of its citizens' claims against Mexico. The war reopened the slavery-extension issue, which had been largely dormant since the Missouri Compromise.

Zachary Taylor emerged as a national hero and succeeded Polk as president in 1849.

MAJOR GENERAL ZACHARY TAYLOR.

WESTWARD EXPANSION

Between the gold rush and the Civil War (1849–1861), Americans in growing numbers filled the Mississippi River valley, Texas, the southwest territories, and the new states of Kansas and Nebraska. During the war, gold and silver discoveries drew prospectors—and later settlers—into Oregon, Colorado, Nevada, Idaho, and Montana.

By 1870 only portions of the Great Plains could truly be called unsettled. For most of the next two decades, that land functioned as the fabled open range, home to cowboys and their grazing cattle from ranches in Texas. But by the late 1880s, with the decline of the range cattle industry, settlers moved in and fenced the Great Plains into family farms. That settlement—and the wild rush of pioneers into the Oklahoma Indian Territory—constituted the last chapter of the westward movement. By the early 1890s, a frontier had ceased to exist within the 48 continental states.

The Oregon Trail

Perhaps some 300,000 to 400,000 people used it during its heyday from the mid-1840s to the late 1860s, and possibly a half million traversed it overall; most completed their journeys from Independence, MO to Oregon City, OR in four to five months. Overwhelmingly, the journey was made by wagons drawn by teams of draft animals. Some people did not have wagons and rode horseback, while others went west with handcarts, animal carts, or even the occasional carriage.

Certainly the notion of Manifest Destiny (coined in the 1840s)—that such expansion was even divinely ordained—played its part, as did the lure for farmers of the fertile and well-watered plain of the Willamette valley (located between Portland and Eugene, Oregon) or, for prospectors, the possibility of striking it rich in the goldfields of California and elsewhere. Many were fleeing economic hardship, especially after the serious panic of the late 1830s, while others, after 1860, were seeking to escape the American Civil War. Still, for a good number of people, going to Oregon was just the latest manifestation of the pioneering instinct that their parents and grandparents had followed before them.

Initially, Independence, Missouri, was the departure point for the Oregon Trail because it was also the eastern terminus of the older Santa Fe Trail. Enterprising individuals quickly recognized that outfitting the overlanders was highly profitable. Soon suppliers had set up shop in St. Joseph, which was farther north and west in Missouri than Independence. Those starting there eliminated some 20 miles (30 km) and several river crossings from the first leg of the trek. The Oregon Trail and the California Trail traced the same route until they split, either at Fort Bridger in southwestern Wyoming or at Soda Springs or the Raft River in southeastern or southern Idaho, respectively. Those heading to Oregon continued northwest, while those traveling to California went southwestward through the deserts of northern Utah and Nevada before crossing the Sierra Nevada range and descending into the Sacramento area of California and beyond.

The California Gold Rush

The first major gold strike in North America occurred near Dahlonega, Georgia, in the late 1820s. It was the impetus for the Indian Removal Act (1830) and led to the Trail of Tears. But the best-known strike occurred at Sutter's Mill, near the Sacramento River in California, in 1848. On January 24 of that year, while John Sutter was having a sawmill built, his carpenter, James W. Marshall, found gold. Sutter and Marshall agreed to become partners, and despite their best efforts to keep their find a secret, they were soon besieged by thousands of fortune seekers who camped out under conditions that only the promise of gold could make them endure. By the following year about 80,000 "forty-niners" (as the fortune seekers of 1849 were called) had stampeded to the California goldfields, and 250,000 of them had made it by 1853. In what was a typical pattern, the gold rush slackened as the most workable deposits were exhausted and organized capital and machinery replaced the efforts of individual miner-adventurers with more efficient and businesslike operations. Likewise, the lawless and violent mining camps gave way to permanent settlements with organized government and law enforcement. Those settlements that lacked other viable economic activities when the gold was exhausted soon became ghost towns.

The California branch of the Oregon Trail was especially popular in the late 1840s and early 1850s, as hordes of gold seekers joined the gold rush to California.

Like statistics on the total number of emigrants who traveled the Oregon Trail, estimates of how many people died en route have varied considerably. Low-end figures on mortality tend to be around 4 to 6 percent of the total (i.e., some 12,000 to 24,000 deaths), and estimates range up to 10 percent.

Whatever the reason those intrepid individuals made the trek West for, the overland journey tended to be the defining experience in their lives. Furthermore, their journeys affected the lives of the thousands who followed them, for the settlement of the American West was opened by those pioneers, and it was they who led the way in molding and unifying the country.

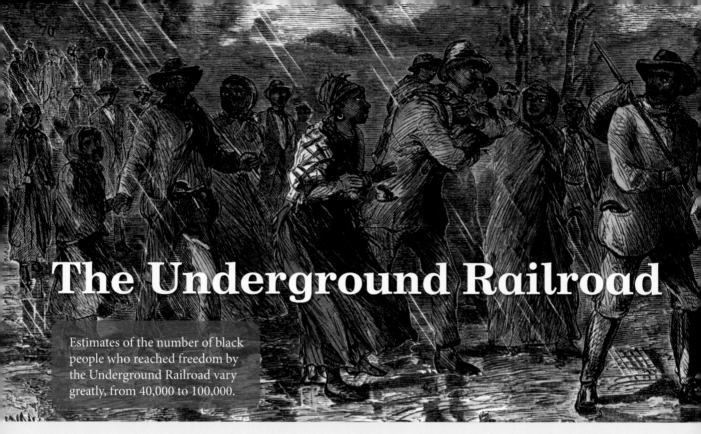

The Underground Railroad

Estimates of the number of black people who reached freedom by the Underground Railroad vary greatly, from 40,000 to 100,000.

The Underground Railroad was a system existing in the Northern states before the Civil War by which escaped slaves from the South were secretly helped by sympathetic Northerners, in defiance of the Fugitive Slave Acts, to reach places of safety in the North or in Canada. Though neither underground nor a railroad, it was thus named because its activities had to be carried out in secret, using darkness or disguise, and because railway terms were used in reference to the conduct of the system. Various routes were lines, stopping places were called stations, those who aided along the way were conductors, and their charges were known as packages or freight. The network of routes extended in all directions throughout 14 Northern states and "the promised land" of Canada, which was beyond the reach of fugitive-slave hunters. Those who most actively assisted slaves to escape by way of the "railroad" were members of the free black community (including such former slaves as Harriet Tubman), Northern abolitionists, philanthropists, and such church leaders as Quaker Thomas Garrett. Harriet Beecher Stowe, famous for her novel *Uncle Tom's Cabin*, gained firsthand knowledge of fugitive slaves through her contact with the Underground Railroad in Cincinnati, Ohio.

The Fugitive Slave Acts

The 1793 Fugitive Slave Acts enforced Article IV, Section 2, of the U.S. Constitution in authorizing any federal district judge or circuit court judge, or any state magistrate, to decide finally and without a jury trial the status of an alleged fugitive slave. The measure met with strong opposition in the Northern states, some of which enacted personal-liberty laws to hamper the execution of the federal law; these laws provided that fugitives who appealed from an original decision against them were entitled to a jury trial. As early as 1810 individual dissatisfaction with the law of 1793 had taken the form of systematic assistance rendered to black slaves escaping from the South to New England or Canada—via the Underground Railroad. The demand from the South for more effective legislation resulted in enactment of a second Fugitive Slave Act in 1850. Under this law fugitives could not testify on their own behalf, nor were they permitted a trial by jury. Heavy penalties were imposed upon federal marshals who refused to enforce the law or from whom a fugitive escaped; penalties were also imposed on individuals who helped slaves to escape.

Under the second Fugitive Slave Act in 1850, special commissioners were to have concurrent jurisdiction with the U.S. courts in enforcing the law. The severity of the 1850 measure led to abuses and defeated its purpose. The number of abolitionists increased, the operations of the Underground Railroad became more efficient, and new personal-liberty laws were enacted in many Northern states.

Harriet Tubman

Born a slave in 1820, Araminta Ross later adopted her mother's first name, Harriet. From early childhood she worked variously as a maid, a nurse, a field hand, a cook, and a woodcutter. About 1844 she married John Tubman, a free black.

In 1849, on the strength of rumours that she was about to be sold, Tubman fled to Philadelphia, leaving behind her husband, parents, and siblings. In December 1850 she made her way to Baltimore, Maryland, whence she led her sister and two children to freedom. That journey was the first of some 19 increasingly dangerous forays into Maryland in which, over the next decade, she conducted upward of 300 fugitive slaves along the Underground Railroad to Canada.

By her extraordinary courage, ingenuity, persistence, and iron discipline, which she enforced upon her charges, Tubman became the railroad's most famous conductor and was known as the "Moses of her people." It has been said that she never lost a fugitive she was leading to freedom. Rewards offered by slaveholders for Tubman's capture eventually totaled $40,000. Abolitionists, however, celebrated her courage.

From 1862 to 1865 Tubman served as a scout, as well as nurse and laundress, for Union forces in South Carolina. For the Second Carolina Volunteers, under the command of Col. James Montgomery, Tubman spied on Confederate territory. When she returned with information about the locations of warehouses and ammunition, Montgomery's troops were able to make carefully planned attacks.

ABOLITIONISM

Despite its brutality and inhumanity, the slave system aroused little protest until the 18th century, when rationalist thinkers of the Enlightenment began to criticize it for its violation of the rights of man, and Quaker and other evangelical religious groups condemned it for its un-Christian qualities. By the late 18th century, moral disapproval of slavery was widespread, and antislavery reformers won a number of deceptively easy victories during this period. In the United States, all of the states north of Maryland abolished slavery between 1777 and 1804. But antislavery sentiments had little effect on the centers of slavery themselves: the great plantations of the Deep South, the West Indies, and South America. Turning their attention to these areas, British and American abolitionists began working in the late 18th century to prohibit the importation of African slaves into the British colonies and the United States. The United States prohibited the importation of slaves that same year, though widespread smuggling continued until about 1862.

Antislavery forces then concentrated on winning the emancipation of those populations already in slavery. Slavery had gained new vitality when an extremely profitable cotton-based agriculture developed in the South in the early 19th century. Reacting to abolitionist attacks that branded its "peculiar institution" as brutal and immoral, the South had intensified its system of slave control, particularly after the Nat Turner revolt of 1831. By that time, American abolitionists realized the failure of gradualism and persuasion, and they subsequently turned to a more militant policy, demanding immediate abolition by law.

William Lloyd Garrison

In 1829, with pioneer abolitionist Benjamin Lundy, William Lloyd Garrison became co-editor of the *Genius of Universal Emancipation* in Baltimore; he also served a short term in jail for libeling a Newburyport merchant who was engaged in the coastal slave trade. Released in June 1830, Garrison returned to Boston and, a year later, established *The Liberator*, which became known as the most uncompromising of American antislavery journals.

Through *The Liberator*, which circulated widely both in England and the United States, Garrison soon achieved recognition as the most radical of American antislavery advocates. In 1832 he founded the New England Anti-Slavery Society, the first immediatist society in the country, and in 1833 he helped organize the American Anti-Slavery Society, writing its Declaration of Sentiments and serving as its first corresponding secretary. It was primarily as an editorialist, however, excoriating slave owners and their moderate opponents alike, that he became known and feared. "If those who deserve the lash feel it and wince at it," he wrote in explaining his refusal to alter his harsh tone, "I shall be assured that I am striking the right persons in the right place."

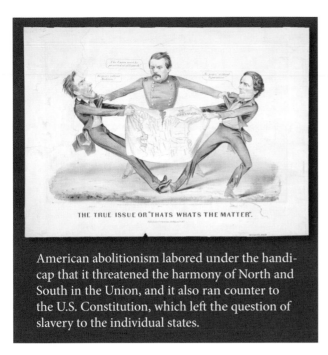

THE TRUE ISSUE OR "THATS WHATS THE MATTER".

American abolitionism labored under the handicap that it threatened the harmony of North and South in the Union, and it also ran counter to the U.S. Constitution, which left the question of slavery to the individual states.

The American Anti-Slavery Society

As the main activist arm of the Abolition Movement, the Anti-Slavery Society was founded in 1833 under the leadership of William Lloyd Garrison. By 1840 its auxiliary societies numbered 2,000, with a total membership ranging from 150,000 to 200,000. The societies sponsored meetings, adopted resolutions, signed antislavery petitions to be sent to Congress, published journals and enlisted subscriptions, printed and distributed propaganda in vast quantities, and sent out agents and lecturers (70 in 1836 alone) to carry the antislavery message to Northern audiences.

In 1839 the national organization split over basic differences of approach: Garrison and his followers were more radical than other members; they denounced the U.S. Constitution as supportive of slavery and insisted on sharing organizational responsibility with women. The less radical wing, led by the Tappan brothers, formed the American and Foreign Anti-Slavery Society, which advocated moral suasion and political action and led directly to the birth of the Liberty Party in 1840. Because of this cleavage in national leadership, the bulk of the activity in the 1840s and 1850s was carried on by state and local societies. The antislavery issue entered the mainstream of American politics through the Free-Soil Party (1848–54) and subsequently the Republican Party (founded in 1854).

Frederick Douglass

Born in 1818 and separated as an infant from his slave mother (he never knew his white father), Frederick lived with his grandmother on a Maryland plantation until, at age eight, his owner sent him to Baltimore to live as a house servant with the family of Hugh Auld, whose wife defied state law by teaching the boy to read. Frederick tried to escape with three others in 1833, but the plot was discovered before they could get away. Five years later, however, he fled to New York City and then to New Bedford, Massachusetts, where he worked as a laborer for three years, eluding slave hunters by changing his surname to Douglass.

At a Nantucket, Massachusetts, antislavery convention in 1841, Douglass was invited to describe his feelings and experiences under slavery. These extemporaneous remarks were so poignant and eloquent that he was unexpectedly catapulted into a new career as agent for the Massachusetts Anti-Slavery Society. From then on, despite heckling and mockery, insult, and violent personal attack, Douglass never flagged in his devotion to the abolitionist cause.

THE CIVIL WAR

The secession of the Southern states in 1860–61 and the ensuing outbreak of armed hostilities were the culmination of decades of growing sectional friction over slavery. Although agriculture—mostly smaller farms that relied on free labor—remained the dominant sector in the North, industrialization had taken root there. By contrast, the Southern economy was based principally on large farms (plantations) that produced commercial crops such as cotton and that relied on slaves as the main labor force. Rather than invest in factories or railroads as Northerners had done, Southerners invested their money in slaves—even more than in land; by 1860, 84 percent of the capital invested in manufacturing was invested in the free (nonslaveholding) states. Also by 1860 the per capita wealth of Southern whites was twice that of Northerners, and three-fifths of the wealthiest individuals in the country were Southerners.

The extension of slavery into new territories and states had been an issue as far back as the Northwest Ordinance of 1784. When the slave territory of Missouri sought statehood in 1818, Congress debated for two years before arriving upon the Missouri Compromise of 1820. This was the first of a series of political deals that resulted from arguments between pro-slavery and antislavery forces over the expansion of the "peculiar institution," as it was known, into the West. More and more Northerners, driven by a sense of morality or an interest in protecting free labor, came to believe, in the 1850s, that bondage needed to be eradicated. White Southerners feared that limiting the expansion of slavery would consign the institution to certain death. Over the course of the decade, the two sides became increasingly polarized and politicians less able to contain the dispute through compromise. When Abraham Lincoln, the candidate of the explicitly antislavery Republican Party, won the 1860 presidential election, seven Southern states (South Carolina, Mississippi, Florida, Alabama, Georgia, Louisiana, and Texas) carried out their threat and seceded, organizing as the Confederate States of America.

In the early morning hours of April 12, 1861, rebels opened fire on Fort Sumter, at the entrance to the harbor of Charleston, South Carolina. Curiously, this first encounter of what would be the bloodiest war in the history of the United States claimed no victims.

The War Begins

After a 34-hour bombardment at Fort Sumter, Maj. Robert Anderson surrendered his command of about 85 soldiers to some 5,500 besieging Confederate troops under P.G.T. Beauregard. Within weeks, four more Southern states (Virginia, Arkansas, Tennessee, and North Carolina)

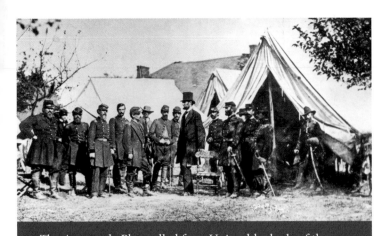

The Anaconda Plan called for a Union blockade of the Confederacy's coastline as well as a decisive thrust down the Mississippi River and an ensuing strangulation of the South by Federal land and naval forces. But it was to take four years of grim, unrelenting warfare and enormous casualties and devastation before the Confederates could be defeated and the Union preserved.

left the Union to join the Confederacy. With war upon the land, President Lincoln called for 75,000 militiamen to serve for three months. He proclaimed a naval blockade of the Confederate states, although he insisted that they did not legally constitute a sovereign country but were instead states in rebellion. He also directed the secretary of the treasury to advance $2 million to assist in the raising of troops, and he suspended the writ of habeas corpus, first along the East Coast and ultimately throughout the country. The Confederate government had previously authorized a call for 100,000 soldiers for at least six months' service, and this figure was soon increased to 400,000.

Robert E. Lee

As commander in chief of Virginia's rebellion forces, Lee saw it as his first task to concentrate troops, armaments, and equipment at major points where the invasion might be expected. During this period, Confederate troops joined the Virginia forces and subdued the Federal Army at the first Battle of Bull Run (July 21, 1861). The attempt at a quick suppression of the Southern states was over and, as Lee was one of the first to realize, a long, all-out war began. Between July 1861 and June 1862, Confederate president Jefferson Davis appointed Lee to several unrewarding positions, the last of which was the trying post of military adviser to the president. Here, however, Lee, working independently of Davis, was able to introduce a coherent strategy into the Confederacy's defense.

Ulysses S. Grant

Grant was appointed lieutenant general in March 1864 and was entrusted with command of all the U.S. armies. His basic plan for the 1864 campaign was to immobilize the army of General Robert E. Lee near the Confederate capital at Richmond, Virginia, while General William Tecumseh Sherman led the western Union army southward through Georgia. It worked. By mid-June, Lee was pinned down at Petersburg, near Richmond, while Sherman's army cut and rampaged through Georgia and cavalry forces under General Philip Sheridan destroyed railroads and supplies in Virginia. On April 2, 1865, Lee was forced to abandon his Petersburg defensive line, and the surrender of Lee's army followed on April 9 at Appomattox Court House. This surrender, in effect, marked the end of the Civil War.

THE CIVIL WAR

The first military operations took place in northwestern Virginia, where non-slaveholding pro-Union Virginians sought to secede from the Confederacy. Gen. George B. McClellan, in command of Federal forces in southern Ohio, advanced on his own initiative in the early summer of 1861 into western Virginia with about 20,000 men. He encountered smaller forces sent there by Lee, who was then in Richmond in command of all Virginia troops. Although showing signs of occasional hesitation, McClellan quickly won three small but significant battles: on June 3 at Philippi, on July 11 at Rich Mountain, and on July 13 at Carrick's Ford. McClellan's casualties were light, and his victories went far toward eliminating Confederate resistance in northwestern Virginia, which had refused to recognize secession, and toward paving the way for the admittance into the Union of the new state of West Virginia in 1863.

The year 1862 marked a major turning point in the war, especially the war in the East, as Lee took command of the Confederate army, which he promptly renamed the Army of Northern Virginia. With Lee's ascent the Army of the Potomac found itself repeatedly battered. While the Army of the Potomac was beleaguered by less-than-visionary leadership, Union forces in the West experienced far greater success under more-aggressive generals. Paradoxically, Lee kept the Confederate war effort going long enough for Lincoln to issue the Emancipation Proclamation, which struck at the very institution the South had gone to war to protect.

The enormous death rate—roughly 2 percent of the 1860 population of the U.S. died in the war—had an enormous impact on American society. Americans were deeply religious, and they struggled to understand how a benevolent God could allow such destruction to go on for so long.

The Emancipation Proclamation

From the outset of the war, slaves had been pouring into Federal camps seeking safety and freedom. Early in the war, Lincoln had slapped the wrists of commanders who tried to issue emancipation edicts in areas under their control. Trying to balance political and military necessity against moral imperatives, Lincoln believed that keeping the slave-owning border states—Maryland, Delaware, Missouri, and particularly Kentucky—in the Union was critical and that making any move toward freeing slaves could incite those states to secede. Moreover, the Constitution protected slavery in several ways, most importantly through its defense of property rights. Finally, Lincoln believed for the first year or so of the war that a significant number of Unionists existed in the seceded states and that, given time, those people would rise up and revolt against the Confederate government.

In its final form, the Emancipation Proclamation would free the slaves in areas that were not under Union control as of January 1, 1863, when it went into effect. This meant it did not apply in the border states or places such as New Orleans, which were already under Union military occupation by that time. Lincoln realized that such a move would strike a serious blow militarily to the Confederates, who relied on bondsmen for the bulk of their labor during the war, by both demoralizing white Southerners and giving additional incentive to slaves to run away.

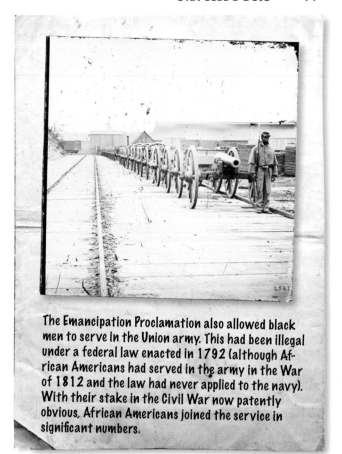

The Emancipation Proclamation also allowed black men to serve in the Union army. This had been illegal under a federal law enacted in 1792 (although African Americans had served in the army in the War of 1812 and the law had never applied to the navy). With their stake in the Civil War now patently obvious, African Americans joined the service in significant numbers.

The Cost and Significance of the War

The triumph of the North, above and beyond its superior naval forces, numbers, and industrial and financial resources, was partly due to the statesmanship of Lincoln, who by 1864 had become a masterful political and war leader, to the pervading valour of Federal soldiers, and to the increasing skill of their officers. The victory can also be attributed in part to failures of Confederate transportation, matériel, and political leadership.

Some have called the American Civil War the last of the old-fashioned wars; others have termed it the first modern war. There were many innovations. It was the first war in history in which ironclad warships clashed; the first in which the telegraph and railroad played significant roles; the first to use, extensively, rifled ordnance and shell guns and to introduce a machine gun (the Gatling gun); the first to have widespread newspaper coverage, voting by servicemen in the field in national elections, and photographic recordings.

Traditionally, historians have put war deaths at about 360,000 for the Union and 260,000 for the Confederates. In the second decade of the 21st century, however, a demographer used better data and more sophisticated tools to convincingly revise the total death toll upward to 752,000 and indicated that it could be as high as 851,000.

Reconstruction

Reconstruction(1865–77) followed the American Civil War and attempted to redress the inequities of slavery and its political, social, and economic legacy and to solve the problems arising from the readmission to the Union of the 11 states that had seceded at or before the outbreak of war. The national debate over Reconstruction began during the Civil War. In December 1863, less than a year after he issued the Emancipation Proclamation, Pres. Abraham Lincoln announced the first comprehensive program for Reconstruction, the Ten Percent Plan. Under it, when one-tenth of a state's prewar voters took an oath of loyalty, they could establish a new state government. To Lincoln, the plan was an attempt to weaken the Confederacy rather than a blueprint for the postwar South. It was put into operation in parts of the Union-occupied Confederacy, but none of the new governments achieved broad local support. In 1864 Congress enacted (and Lincoln pocket vetoed) the Wade-Davis Bill, which proposed to delay the formation of new Southern governments until a majority of voters had taken a loyalty oath. Some Republicans were already convinced that equal rights for the former slaves had to accompany the South's readmission to the Union.

Presidential Reconstruction

Following Lincoln's assassination in April 1865, Andrew Johnson became president and inaugurated the period of Presidential Reconstruction (1865–67). Johnson offered a pardon to all Southern whites except Confederate leaders and wealthy planters (although most of these subsequently received individual pardons), restoring their political rights and all property except slaves. He also outlined how new state governments would be created. Apart from the requirement that they abolish slavery, repudiate secession, and abrogate the Confederate debt, these governments were granted a free hand in managing their affairs. They responded by enacting the black codes, laws that required African Americans to sign yearly labor contracts and in other ways sought to limit the freedmen's economic options and reestablish plantation discipline. African Americans strongly resisted the implementation of these measures, and they seriously undermined Northern support for Johnson's policies.

In every state, African Americans formed the overwhelming majority of Southern Republican voters. From the beginning of Reconstruction, black conventions and newspapers throughout the South had called for the extension of full civil and political rights to African Americans.

Radical Reconstruction

Serving an expanded citizenry, Reconstruction governments established the South's first state-funded public school systems, sought to strengthen the bargaining power of plantation laborers, made taxation more equitable, and outlawed racial discrimination in public transportation and accommodations. They also offered lavish aid to railroads and other enterprises in the hope of creating a "New South" whose economic expansion would benefit blacks and whites alike. But the economic program spawned corruption and rising taxes, alienating increasing numbers of white voters.

Meanwhile, the social and economic transformation of the South proceeded apace. To blacks, freedom meant independence from white control. Reconstruction provided the opportunity for African Americans to solidify their family ties and to create independent religious institutions, which became centers of community life that survived long after Reconstruction ended. The former slaves also demanded economic independence. Blacks' hopes that the federal government would provide them with land had been raised by Gen. William T. Sherman's Field Order No. 15 of January 1865, which set aside a large swath of land along the coast of South Carolina and Georgia for the exclusive settlement of black families, and by the Freedmen's Bureau Act of March, which authorized the bureau to rent or sell land in its possession to former slaves. But President Johnson in the summer of 1865 ordered land in federal hands to be returned to its former owners. Lacking land, most former slaves had little economic alternative other than resuming work on plantations owned by whites. Some worked for wages, others as sharecroppers, who divided the crop with the owner at the end of the year. For decades, most Southern blacks remained propertyless and poor.

RECONSTRUCTION OF THE SOUTH.

The political revolution of Reconstruction spawned increasingly violent opposition from white Southerners. White supremacist organizations that committed terrorist acts, such as the Ku Klux Klan, targeted local Republican leaders for beatings or assassination. African Americans who asserted their rights in dealings with white employers, teachers, ministers, and others seeking to assist the former slaves also became targets.

The End of Reconstruction

By the turn of the century, a new racial system had been put in place in the South, resting on the disenfranchisement of black voters, a rigid system of racial segregation, the relegation of African Americans to low-wage agricultural and domestic employment, and legal and extralegal violence to punish those who challenged the new order. Nonetheless, while flagrantly violated, the 14th and 15th amendments remained in the Constitution, waiting to be awakened by subsequent generations who sought to redeem the promise of genuine freedom, citizenry, and suffrage.

Not until the 1960s, in the civil rights movement, sometimes called the "second Reconstruction," would the country again attempt to fulfill the political and social agenda of Reconstruction.

The Expansion of the
RAILROADS

In 1862 Congress authorized the construction of two railroads that together would provide the first railroad link between the Mississippi valley and the Pacific coast. One was the Union Pacific, to run westward from Council Bluffs, Iowa; the other was the Central Pacific, to run eastward from Sacramento, California. To encourage the rapid completion of those roads, Congress provided generous subsidies in the form of land grants and loans. Construction was slower than Congress had anticipated, but the two lines met, with elaborate ceremonies, on May 10, 1869, at Promontory, Utah.

The Union Pacific grew to operate in 13 western states, extending from Council Bluffs, Iowa, and Kansas City, Missouri, to Portland, Oregon, and Los Angeles. Since 1969 it has been owned by the Union Pacific Corporation, a holding company.

In the meantime, other railroads had begun construction westward, but the financial panic of 1873 and the ensuing depression halted or delayed progress on many of those lines. With the return of prosperity after 1877, some railroads resumed or accelerated construction; and by 1883 three more rail connections between the Mississippi valley and the West Coast had been completed—the Northern Pacific, from St. Paul to Portland; the Santa Fe, from Chicago to Los Angeles; and the Southern Pacific, from New Orleans to Los Angeles.

The West developed simultaneously with the building of the western railroads, and in no part of the nation was the importance of railroads more generally recognized. The railroad gave vitality to the regions it served, but, by withholding service, it could doom a community to stagnation. The railroads appeared to be ruthless in exploiting their powerful position: they fixed prices to suit their convenience; they discriminated among their customers; they attempted to gain a monopoly of transportation wherever possible; and they interfered in state and local politics to elect favorites to office, to block unfriendly legislation, and even to influence the decisions of the courts.

To meet its manpower needs, the Central Pacific hired thousands of Chinese laborers, including many recruited from farms in Canton, China. The crew had the formidable task of laying the track that crossed the rugged Sierra Nevada mountain range, blasting nine tunnels to accomplish this. The crew of the Union Pacific, which was composed largely of Irish immigrants and Civil War veterans, had to contend with Indian attacks and the Rocky Mountains.

Central Pacific Railroad

The Central Pacific Railroad was an American railroad company founded in 1861 by a group of California merchants known later as the "Big Four" (Collis P. Huntington, Leland Stanford, Mark Hopkins, and Charles Crocker). The line was first conceived and surveyed by an engineer, Theodore Dehone Judah, who obtained the financial backing of the California group and won federal support in the form of the Pacific Railway Act (1862). The Central Pacific began laying track eastward from Sacremento, California, in 1863.

In subsequent years feeder lines of the Central Pacific were established throughout California, and already existing trackage along southern routes to Texas and New Orleans, Louisiana, was acquired. On March 17, 1884, a new Southern Pacific Company was incorporated to act as a holding company for the several operating railroads; the Central Pacific was leased to it until 1959, when they merged.

The Union Pacific Railroad

The Union Pacific Railroad Company, the company that extended the American railway system to the Pacific Coast, was incorporated by an act of the U.S. Congress on July 1, 1862. The original rail line was built westward 1,006 miles (1,619 km) from Omaha, Nebraska, to meet the Central Pacific, which was being built eastward from Sacramento, California. The two railroads were joined at Promontory, Utah, on May 10, 1869 .

The Union Pacific was largely financed by federal loans and land grants, but it overextended itself through its involvement in the Crédit Mobilier scandal, in which a few manipulators reaped enormous profits. After exposure of the scheme, which left the railroad badly in debt, the company went into receivership in 1893. It was reorganized in 1897 under the leadership of Edward H. Harriman, who was responsible for major improvements and standardization and who led the railroad to participate in the economic development of the West.

With its acquisition of the Southern Pacific Rail Corporation in 1996, Union Pacific became the largest domestic railroad in the United States, controlling almost all of the rail-based shipping in the western two-thirds of the country. It carries products and commodities such as coal, automobiles, foods, forest and agricultural products, and chemicals and is one of the largest intermodal shippers (including truck trailers and containers) in the country.

THE PLAINS WARS

The Plains Wars were a series of conflicts from the early 1850s through the late 1870s between Native Americans and the United States, along with its Indian allies, over control of the Great Plains between the Mississippi River and the Rocky Mountains.

The initial major confrontation, sometimes known as the First Sioux War, broke out in the Dakota Territory near Fort Laramie (in present-day Wyoming) following a dispute over a killed cow between white settlers traveling to the far west and the local Lakota (a Western Sioux group). On August 19, 1854, brevet Second Lieut. John L. Grattan set out from the post with 30 men and two cannons and, after rashly demanding that a far superior Indian force turn over the suspected culprit, he opened fire. In response, the Lakota killed Grattan and his entire assembly. Most Lakota denied the legitimacy of this war, however, effectively isolating those who had been directly involved in the Grattan affair. On September 3, 1855, brevet Brig. Gen. William S. Harney's regulars routed the hostile Lakota at Blue Water Creek (in present-day Nebraska). Although the U.S. Senate failed to ratify the resulting treaty, Harney's blow produced what amounted to a regional armistice.

The following year, open conflict spread southward. Leading about 300 cavalrymen on July 29, 1856, Col. Edwin V. Sumner encountered an equal force of mounted Cheyenne near the south fork of the Solomon River, Kansas Territory. The Cheyenne were eager to engage in battle, assured that magical waters would keep them safe from their white opponents' bullets. As both sides thundered forward, Sumner gave the unusual order for his men to draw their sabers; the stunned Cheyenne, whose medicine did not cover the steel blades, fled in disarray, leading to a period of relative peace in the central Plains.

The Minnesota Massacre

The continuing onslaught of westward-moving white populations and the mismanagement of the reservations by government officials spawned great bitterness among the Dakota, and in August 1862 their most influential leader, Little Crow (Taoyateduta), led attacks that brought the demise of hundreds of white settlers in a single week. The bloodshed sparked a massive backlash, and on September 23 Col. Henry Hastings Sibley handed the Dakota a stinging defeat at the Battle of Wood Lake. Peace factions then regained the ascendancy in many circles, and, as a result, hundreds of those who had been involved in the early attacks were surrendered to the white authorities. The government subsequently hanged 38 Indian prisoners at Mankato.

WHITNEY, **LITTLE CROW,** ST. PAUL.
C. Sioux Chief and Leader of the Indian Massacre of 1862, in Minnesota
Entered according to Act in Congress, by J. E. Whitney, in the year 1862

The Defeat of the Plains Indians

In the northern Plains, growing interest in the Yellowstone River country (now Wyoming and Montana) was upsetting the uneasy peace that had been negotiated at Fort Laramie. Beginning in 1871, government-sponsored surveying expeditions for the Northern Pacific Railroad pressed through the area, some with dozens of scientists and hundreds of military escorts. In 1874 Lieutenant Colonel Gerorge Armstrong Custer's expedition to the Black Hills of present-day South Dakota found traces of gold, and the discovery was confirmed the following year by another team. Amid mounting pressure to secure the region, the Department of the Interior authorized the use of military force in November 1875, paving the way for what some have called the Great Sioux War. An early offensive quickly fizzled, but by May three large army columns were converging on the Yellowstone River valley. Reflecting a consensus view, Maj. Gen. Philip H. Sheridan assured a subordinate of "the impossibility of any large numbers of Indians keeping together as a hostile body for even a week." The greatest risk, he and most others believed, was that the Indians might elude the army's grasp.

Sheridan was wrong, for the Lakota and Cheyenne, inspired by such talented military and spiritual leaders as Crazy Horse and Sitting Bull, had assembled and agreed to fight together. On June 17, 1876, roughly 750 Indians manhandled a column led by one of the army's best officers, Brig. Gen. George Crook, at Rosebud Creek, Montana Territory. Eight days later another detachment met an even bigger defeat at the Little Bighorn, where Custer and nearly half of the 7th Cavalry Regiment were annihilated. Although stunned by the defeat, soldiers soon began combing the region once more. On November 25, Col. Ranald S. Mackenzie's troopers, well supported

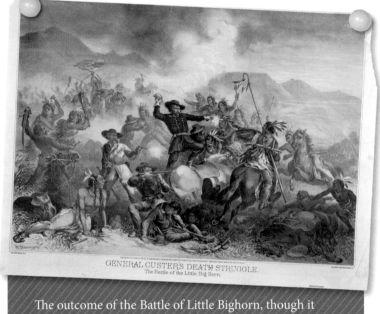

GENERAL CUSTER'S DEATH STRUGGLE.
The Battle of the Little Big Horn.

The outcome of the Battle of Little Bighorn, though it proved to be the height of Indian power, so stunned and enraged white Americans that government troops flooded the area, forcing the Indians to surrender.

by Indian auxiliaries (including Arapaho, Shoshone, Bannock, Pawnee, and some Sioux and Cheyenne), destroyed a large Cheyenne camp at the Red Fork of the Powder River. Expeditions led by Col. Nelson A. Miles maintained the pressure throughout the winter and well into the following year, with the sharpest fights coming at Wolf Mountain (January 8, 1877) and Muddy Creek (May 7). But it was the relentless onslaught and devastating economic blows delivered by the army's field columns, not pitched battles, that most seriously affected Native American resistance. A few hundred Indians fled with Sitting Bull into Canada; the remaining Plains peoples, however, agreed to move to reservations. Desperate attempts by the Cheyenne in the late 1870s to return to their former homelands failed, often with heavy casualties, and the Plains Wars came to a close.

The Civil Rights Cases of 1883

In the last of the great Reconstruction statutes, the Civil Rights Act of 1875, the Republican majority in Congress tried to secure by law some semblance of racial equality that could be protected by the government and by courts. While no one expected that such legislation would change the prevailing racial attitudes held by both Northern and Southern whites, the law aimed to protect African Americans from deprivation of the minimal rights of citizenship.

A critical provision of the Civil Rights Act prohibited racial discrimination in public places, what would later be called "public accommodations," which rested on Section 5 —the enforcement clause—of the Fourteenth Amendment. Five cases testing the application of this section rose in both the North and the South, and the Supreme Court combined them for a single hearing in March 1883. The government argued on behalf of the Civil Rights Act, declaring that the Thirteenth Amendment had not only abolished slavery but conferred all the rights of free citizens on the former slaves and that the Fourteenth Amendment had given Congress the power to protect those rights through appropriate legislation.

The Court disagreed, and, in the opinion for the 8–1 ruling, Justice Joseph P. Bradley denied both of the government's contentions. In effect, the ruling robbed the amendments of much of their meaning. Bradley argued that, because not every example of discrimination against African Americans could be interpreted as a renewal of slavery, the Thirteenth Amendment could not be invoked as a ban on racial prejudice.

Although the Fourteenth Amendment had in fact been drafted specifically to ensure African Americans' rights, Bradley denied that Congress had any affirmative powers under the amendment. Congress could legislate in a remedial manner to correct an unconstitutional law. It could intervene only if a state enacted a law that restricted the rights of African Americans. Bradley also held that if a state failed to take action but, by inaction, tolerated discrimination—such as exclusion from hotels, restaurants, and clubs—Congress could not legislate. By this decision the court in one stroke nullified all congressional power to protect African Americans under the Fourteenth Amendment and left their fate to the states. It also invited the Southern states not only to tolerate but to encourage private discrimination. The ruling would remain in force until the Court disavowed it in upholding the 1964 Civil Rights Act, nearly a century after the Civil War ended.

Opposition to freedom for African Americans often took extralegal forms, notably brutal attacks on former slaves by the Ku Klux Klan.

The Civil War and the Thirteenth Amendment brought an end to slavery in the United States, but they did not give the former bondsmen either legal or political equality. In fact, the Southern states almost immediately passed a series of laws known as "Black Codes," which, though not enslaving the freedmen, severely restricted their freedoms and put them at the mercy of whites.

During the Reconstruction period, Congress tried to protect African Americans through a series of civil rights and enforcement statutes and through two more amendments to the U.S. Constitution. The Fifteenth Amendment declared that the right to vote could not be denied because of race.

The Fourteenth Amendment defined a citizen of the United States as any person born in the country or who had immigrated and been naturalized. It also prohibited the states from denying to any citizen the due process of law or the equal protection of the laws or from abridging the privileges and immunities attached to citizenship.

The Aftermath

The ruling in the Civil Rights Cases not only barred Congress from taking affirmative steps against racial discrimination but permitted states to legally allow private discrimination simply by looking the other way, which they did. In tandem with the landmark decision in *Plessy v. Ferguson* 13 years later, which sanctioned the doctrine of "separate but equal," the Civil Rights Cases inaugurated the Jim Crow era.

SEPARATE but EQUAL

From the late 1870s, Southern state legislatures passed laws requiring the separation of whites from "persons of color" in public transportation and schools, inducting the Jim Crow Era that would last until the 1950s. Generally, anyone of ascertainable or strongly suspected black ancestry in any degree was for that purpose a "person of color"; the pre-Civil War distinction favoring those whose ancestry was known to be mixed—particularly the half-French "free persons of color" in Louisiana—was abandoned. The segregation principle was extended to parks, cemeteries, theatres, and restaurants in an effort to prevent any contact between blacks and whites as equals. It was codified on local and state levels and most famously with the "separate but equal" decision of the U.S. Supreme Court in *Plessy v. Ferguson* (1896).

Prior to the Civil War the inferior status of slaves had made it unnecessary to pass laws segregating them from white people. Both races could work side by side so long as the slave recognized his subordinate place. In the cities, where most free blacks lived, rudimentary forms of segregation existed prior to 1860, but no uniform pattern emerged.

The Separate Car Acts

From 1887 to 1892 nine states, including Louisiana, passed laws requiring separation on public conveyances, such as streetcars and railroads. Though they differed in detail, most of those statutes required equal accommodations for black passengers and imposed fines and even jail terms on railroad employees who did not enforce them. Five of the states also provided criminal fines or imprisonment for passengers who tried to sit in cars from which their race excluded them. The Louisiana Separate Car Act passed in July 1890. In order to "promote the comfort of passengers," railroads had to provide "equal but separate accommodations for the white and colored races" on lines running in the state.

The Louisiana Separate Car Act marked a dramatic and humiliating reversal of fortune for the black and mixed-race citizens of Louisiana. Although a slave state, Louisiana in general and New Orleans in particular had always had, because of their French origins, a more-tolerant attitude toward people of color than did other Deep South states. In addition to the usual demarcation between black and white, since the 1700s New Orleans had acknowledged a third class, free people of color, sometimes called Creoles, the freed descendants of European fathers and African mothers who had enjoyed a great deal of autonomy. Although Louisiana, like most Southern states, had laws against marriage between slaves, it did allow free people of color to marry, testify in court, and in some cases inherit property from their fathers. Some became slaveowners themselves, and apparently many of them accumulated significant property. Their social standing, especially in New Orleans, had insulated them from some of the white reaction following the war. But when whites regained power after the end of Reconstruction, they saw only two races, and the privileged position of the free people of color evaporated; from then on they were black as far as the law was concerned.

In the Civil Rights Cases of 1883, the court overturned key elements of the Civil Rights Act of 1875, thereby sanctioning the notion of "separate but equal" facilities and transportation for the races.

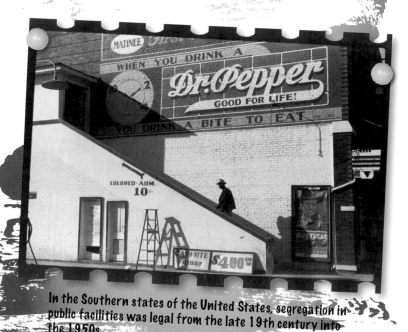

In the Southern states of the United States, segregation in public facilities was legal from the late 19th century into the 1950s.

The Homer Plessy Case

On June 7, 1892, Homer Plessy walked into the Press Street Depot in New Orleans, bought a first-class ticket to Covington, and boarded the East Louisiana Railroad's Number 8 train. As the train pulled away from the station, the conductor asked the light-complected Plessy if he was a "colored man." Plessy said he was and the conductor told him to move to the colored car. Homer Plessy refused. "I am an American citizen," he told the trainman. "I have paid for a first-class ticket, and intend to ride to Covington in the first-class car." The conductor stopped the train, and Detective Christopher Cain boarded the car, arrested Plessy, and forcibly dragged him off the train with the help of a few other passengers. After a night in jail, Plessy appeared in criminal court before Judge John Howard Ferguson to answer charges of violating the Separate Car Act.

The Committee to Test the Constitutionality of the Separate Car Act then posted a $500 bond so Plessy could be released. Plessy was not arraigned until October 1892, and once again his trio of attorneys—Louis A. Martinet, James Walker, and Albion W Tourgée—entered a plea claiming that the act was unconstitutional and therefore the court did not have jurisdiction to hear or determine the facts.

Plessy failed in court, and his subsequent appeal to the state Supreme Court was similarly unsuccessful. An appeal to the U.S. Supreme Court followed, but time was hardly on Plessy's side. Throughout the country, but especially in the South, conditions for African Americans were quickly deteriorating. The Supreme Court ruling that followed on May 18, 1896, and that bore the names of Plessy and Ferguson solidified the establishment of the Jim Crow era.

WOMEN'S SUFFRAGE

From the founding of the United States, women were almost universally excluded from voting. Only when women began to chafe at this restriction, however, was their exclusion made explicit. The movement for woman suffrage started in the early 19th century during the agitation against slavery. Women such as Lucretia Mott showed a keen interest in the antislavery movement and proved to be admirable public speakers. When Elizabeth Cady Stanton joined the antislavery forces, she and Mott agreed that the rights of women, as well as those of slaves, needed redress. In July 1848 they issued a call for a convention to discuss the issue of women's rights; this convention met in Stanton's hometown, Seneca Falls, New York, on July 19–20, 1848, and issued a declaration that called for woman suffrage and for the right of women to educational and employment opportunities. It was followed in 1850 by the first national convention of the women's movement, held in Worcester, Massachusetts, by Lucy Stone and a group of prominent eastern suffragists. Another convention, held in Syracuse, New York, in 1852, was the occasion of the first joint venture between Stanton and the dynamic suffragist leader Susan B. Anthony; together these two figures led the American suffragist movement for the next 50 years.

Other woman suffrage conventions were held as the movement gained its first mass strength, but at first no way of extending the vote to women was known except by amendments to the constitutions of the various states. Several attempts were made in this regard after the American Civil War (1861–65), but even though the Territory of Wyoming granted women the right to vote in all elections in 1869, it soon became apparent that an amendment of the federal Constitution would be a preferable plan. Accordingly, the National Woman Suffrage Association was formed in 1869 with the declared object of securing the ballot for women by an amendment to the Constitution. Anthony and Stanton were the leaders of this organization, which held a convention every year for 50 years after its founding. In 1869 another organization, the American Woman Suffrage Association, was founded by Lucy Stone with the aim of securing woman suffrage by obtaining amendments to that effect in the constitutions of the various

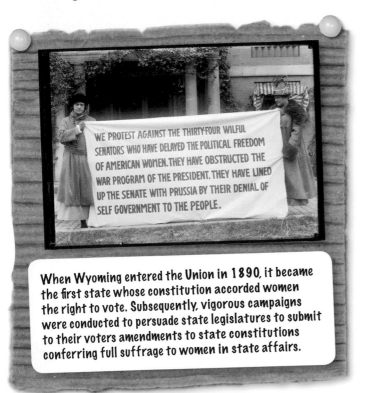

When Wyoming entered the Union in 1890, it became the first state whose constitution accorded women the right to vote. Subsequently, vigorous campaigns were conducted to persuade state legislatures to submit to their voters amendments to state constitutions conferring full suffrage to women in state affairs.

states. In 1890 the two organizations united under the name National American Woman Suffrage Association and worked together for almost 30 years.

A Win for Women's Suffrage

World War I, and the major role played in it by women in various capacities, broke down most of the remaining opposition to woman suffrage in the United States. Amendments to the federal Constitution concerning woman suffrage had been introduced into Congress in 1878 and 1914, but the 1878 amendment had been overwhelmingly defeated, and the 1914 amendment had narrowly failed to gain even a simple majority of the votes in thc House of Representatives and the Senate (a two-thirds majority vote in Congress was needed for the amendment to be sent to the state legislatures for ratification). By 1918, however, both major political parties were committed to woman suffrage, and the amendment was carried by the necessary two-thirds majorities in both the House and Senate in January 1918 and June 1919.

After Wyoming entered the Union, efforts were also made to give women the right to vote in presidential elections and, in some states, the right to vote in municipal and local elections. In the next 25 years various individual states yielded to the movement's demands and enfranchised their women; each such state increased the members of Congress elected partly by women.

Vigorous campaigns were then waged to secure ratification of the amendment by two-thirds of the state legislatures, and on August 18, 1920, Tennessee became the 36th state to ratify the amendment. On August 26 the Nineteenth Amendment was proclaimed by the secretary of state as being part of the Constitution of the United States. Women in the United States were enfranchised on an equal basis with men. The text reads as follows:

"The right of citizens of the United States to vote shall not be denied or abridged by the United States or by any State on account of sex. Congress shall have power to enforce this article by appropriate legislation."

Members of Congress elected by women were partly obliged by the nature of their constituency to vote for a woman suffrage amendment to the United States Constitution. By 1918 women had acquired equal suffrage with men in 15 states.

The Spanish-American War

The Spanish-American War was a conflict between the U.S. and Spain which ended Spain's colonial rule in the Americas, originating from the Cuban struggle for independence from Spain in 1895. Spain's brutally repressive measures to halt the rebellion were graphically portrayed for the U.S. public by several sensational newspapers, and American sympathy for the rebels rose. The growing popular demand for U.S. intervention became an insistent chorus after the unexplained sinking in Havana harbor of the battleship *USS Maine* (Feb. 15, 1898), which had been sent to protect U.S. citizens and property after anti-Spanish rioting in Havana. Spain announced an armistice on April 9 and speeded up its new program to grant Cuba limited powers of self-government, but the U.S. Congress soon afterward issued resolutions that declared Cuba's right to independence, demanded the withdrawal of Spain's armed forces from the island, and authorized the President's use of force to secure that withdrawal while renouncing any U.S. design for annexing Cuba.

Spain declared war on the United States on April 24, 1898, followed by a U.S. declaration of war on the 25th, which was made retroactive to April 21. The ensuing war was pathetically one-sided, since Spain had readied neither its army nor its navy for a distant war with the formidable power of the United States. Commodore George Dewey led a U.S. naval squadron into Manila Bay in the Philippines on May 1, 1898, and destroyed the anchored Spanish fleet in a leisurely morning engagement, in which only seven American seamen were wounded. Manila itself was occupied by U.S. troops by August.

When war was declared in 1898, Theodore Roosevelt organized the 1st Volunteer Cavalry, known as the Rough Riders, who were sent to fight in Cuba. Roosevelt was a brave and well-publicized military leader. The charge of the Rough Riders (on foot) up Kettle Hill during the Battle of Santiago made him the biggest national hero to come out of the Spanish-American War.

The Battle of Santiago

The elusive Spanish Caribbean fleet under Adm. Pascual Cervera was located in Santiago harbor in Cuba by U.S. reconnaissance. An army of regular troops and volunteers under Gen. William Shafter (and including Theodore Roosevelt and his 1st Volunteer Cavalry, the "Rough Riders") landed on the coast east of Santiago and slowly advanced on the city in an effort to force Cervera's fleet out of the harbor. Cervera led his squadron out of Santiago on July 3, 1898, and tried to escape westward along the coast. In the ensuing battle all of his ships came under heavy fire from U.S. guns and were beached in a burning or sinking condition. Santiago surrendered to Shafter on July 17, thus effectively ending the war.

THE SPANISH-AMERICAN TREATY OF PEACE, PARIS DEC. 10TH 1898.

A New Stake in Politics

By the Treaty of Paris (signed Dec. 10, 1898), Spain renounced all claim to Cuba, ceded Guam and Puerto Rico to the United States, and transferred sovereignty over the Philippines to the United States for $20 million. The Spanish-American War was an important turning point in the history of both antagonists. Spain's defeat decisively turned the nation's attention away from its overseas colonial adventures and inward upon its domestic needs, a process that led to both a cultural and a literary renaissance and two decades of much-needed economic development in Spain. The victorious United States, on the other hand, emerged from the war a world power with far-flung overseas possessions and a new stake in international politics that would soon lead it to play a determining role in the affairs of Europe.

In January 1898, partly as a conciliatory gesture to the Spanish authorities there and partly to protect the lives and property of U.S. citizens presumably endangered by recent riots, the *Maine* was sent to Havana harbor. On February 15 an explosion sank the ship, carrying 260 seamen to their deaths. The exact cause of the disaster was never firmly established, though Spain offered to submit the question of its responsibility to arbitration.

The Industrialization of the U.S.

By 1878 the United States had reentered a period of prosperity after a long depression in the mid-1870s. In the ensuing 20 years the volume of industrial production, the number of workers employed in industry, and the number of manufacturing plants all more than doubled. A more accurate index to the scope of this industrial advance may be found in the aggregate annual value of all manufactured goods, which increased from about $5,400,000,000 in 1879 to perhaps $13,000,000,000 in 1899. The expansion of the iron and steel industry, always a key factor in any industrial economy, was even more impressive: from 1880 to 1900 the annual production of steel in the United States went from about 1,400,000 to more than 11,000,000 tons. Before the end of the century, the United States surpassed Great Britain in the production of iron and steel and was providing more than one-quarter of the world's supply of pig iron.

Two-thirds of the iron and steel industry was concentrated in the area of western Pennsylvania and eastern Ohio. After 1880, however, the development of iron mines in northern Minnesota and in Tennessee and northern Alabama was followed by the expansion of the iron and steel industry in the Chicago area and by the establishment of steel mills in northern Alabama and in Tennessee.

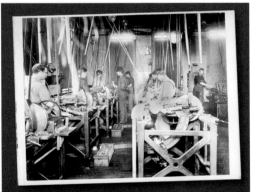

The first effective labor organization that was more than regional in membership and influence was the Knights of Labor, organized in 1869. The Knights believed in the unity of the interests of all producing groups and sought to enlist in their ranks not only all laborers but everyone who could be truly classified as a producer.

Paving the Way Towards Industry

Many factors combined to produce this burst of industrial activity. The exploitation of Western resources, including mines and lumber, stimulated a demand for improved transportation, while the gold and silver mines provided new sources of capital for investment in the East. The construction of railroads, especially in the West and South, with the resulting demand for steel rails, was a major force in the expansion of the steel industry and increased the railroad mileage in the United States from less than 93,262 miles in 1880 to about 190,000 miles in 1900. Technological advances, including the utilization of the Bessemer and open-hearth processes in the manufacture of steel, resulted in improved products and lower production costs. A series of major inventions, including the telephone, typewriter, linotype, phonograph, electric light, cash register, air brake, refrigerator car, and the automobile, became the bases for new industries, while many of them revolutionized the conduct of business. The use of petroleum products in industry as well as for domestic heating and lighting became the cornerstone of the most powerful of the new industries of the period, while the trolley car, the increased use of gas and electric power, and the telephone led to the establishment of important public utilities that were natural monopolies and could operate only on the basis of franchises granted by state or municipal governments. The widespread employment of the corporate form of business organization offered new opportunities for large-scale financing of business enterprise and attracted new capital, much of it furnished by European investors. Yet, the expansion of industry was accompanied by increased tensions between employers and workers and by the appearance, for the first time in the United States, of national labor unions. The year 1886 was a troubled one in labor relations. There were nearly 1,600 strikes, involving about 600,000 workers, with the eight-hour day the most prominent item in the demands of labor. Many these strikes were called for May Day; some of them were successful, but the failure of others and internal conflicts between skilled and unskilled members led to a decline in the Knights of Labor's popularity and influence.

The Haymarket Riot

The most serious blow to the U.S. labor movement came from a tragic occurrence with which they were only indirectly associated. One of the strikes called for May Day in 1886 was against the McCormick Harvesting Machine Company in Chicago. Fighting broke out along the picket lines on May 3, and, when police intervened to restore order, several strikers were injured or killed. Union leaders called a protest meeting at Haymarket Square for the evening of May 4; but, as the meeting was breaking up, a group of anarchists took over and began to make inflammatory speeches. The police quickly intervened, and a bomb exploded, killing seven policemen and injuring many others. Eight of the anarchists were arrested, tried, and convicted of murder. Four of them were hanged, and one committed suicide. The remaining three were pardoned in 1893 by Gov. John P. Altgeld, who was persuaded that they had been convicted in such an atmosphere of prejudice that it was impossible to be certain that they were guilty.

The public tended to blame organized labor for the Haymarket tragedy, and many persons had become convinced that the activities of unions were likely to be attended by violence.

The Progressive Movement
at the Turn of the 20th Century

Roosevelt relished the power of the office and viewed the presidency as an outlet for his unbounded energy. He was a proud and fervent nationalist who willingly bucked the passive Jeffersonian tradition of fearing the rise of a strong chief executive and a powerful central government.

In 1901 the reform upheavel—which focused on objectives like regulating railroads and public utilities, preventing child labor, protecting women workers, expanding charitable services, and providing adequate worker's compensation—was too strong to be contained within state boundaries. Moreover, certain problems with which only the federal government was apparently competent to deal cried out for solution. President McKinley might have succeeded in ignoring the rising tide of public opinion had he served out his second term, but McKinley's assassination in September 1901 brought to the presidency an entirely different kind of man—Theodore Roosevelt, at age 42 the youngest man yet to enter the White House. Roosevelt had broad democratic sympathies; moreover, thanks to his experience as police commissioner of New York City and governor of New York state, he was the first president to have an intimate knowledge of modern urban problems. Because Congress was securely controlled by a group of archconservative Republicans, the new president had to feel his way cautiously in legislative matters, but he emerged full-grown as a tribune of the people after his triumph in the presidential election of 1904. By 1906 he was the undisputed spokesman of national progressivism and by far its best publicity agent. (The White House was, he said, "a bully pulpit.")

Roosevelt's Crackdown on Industry

In 1901, Americans were perhaps most alarmed about the spread of so-called trusts, or industrial combinations, which they thought were responsible for the steady price increases that had occurred each year since 1897. Alert to the winds of public opinion, Roosevelt responded by activating the Sherman Antitrust Act of 1890, legislation enacted by the United States Congress to curb concentrations of power that interfere with trade and reduce economic competition,

Using the same tactics of aggressive leadership, Roosevelt in 1906 obtained passage of a Meat Inspection Act and a Pure Food and Drug Act. Passage of each was aided by the publication of Upton Sinclair's famous novel, *The Jungle* (1906), which revealed in gory detail the unsanitary conditions of the Chicago stockyards and meat-packing plants.

which had lain dormant because of successive presidents' refusal to enforce it.

Beginning in 1902 with a suit to dissolve a northwestern railroad monopoly, Roosevelt moved next against the so-called Beef Trust, then against the oil, tobacco, and other monopolies. In every case the Supreme Court supported the administration. In addition, in 1903 Roosevelt persuaded a reluctant Congress to establish a Bureau of Corporations with sweeping power to investigate business practices; the bureau's thoroughgoing reports were of immense assistance in antitrust cases. While establishing the supremacy of the federal government in the industrial field, Roosevelt in 1902 also took action unprecedented in the history of the presidency by intervening on labor's behalf to force the arbitration of a strike by the United Mine Workers of America against the Pennsylvania anthracite coal operators.

Protecting the Land

Meanwhile, almost from his accession to the presidency, Roosevelt had been carrying on a crusade, often independent of Congress, to conserve the nation's fast-dwindling natural resources and to make them available for exploitation under rigorous national supervision. He withdrew from the public domain some 148,000,000 acres of forest lands, 80,000,000 acres of mineral lands, and 1,500,000 acres of water-power sites. Moreover, adoption of the National Reclamation Act of 1902 made possible the beginning of an ambitious federal program of irrigation and hydroelectric development in the West.

Upton Sinclair's *The Jungle*

The most famous, influential, and enduring of all muckraking novels, *The Jungle* was an exposé of conditions in the Chicago stockyards. Because of public response, legislation was passed and conditions in the slaughterhouses were improved.

The novel was written when Sinclair was sent by the socialist weekly newspaper *Appeal to Reason* to investigate working conditions in the meatpacking industry. He wrote pointedly about the exploitation of immigrant laborers and graphically described the disguising of spoiled and diseased meat and the unsanitary environment in the stockyards. Although Sinclair's chief goal was to expose abusive labor conditions, the American public was most horrified by the lack of sanitation in the meat-processing plants.

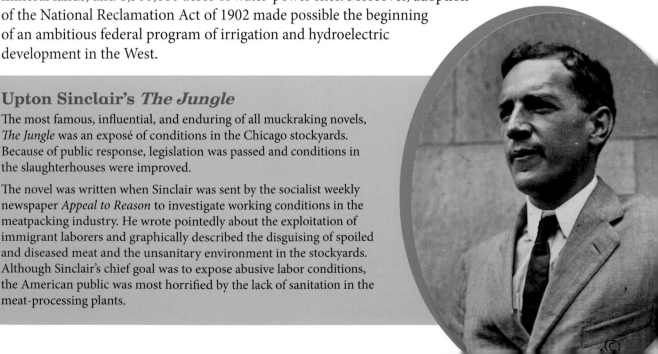

Origins of the NATIONAL PARK SERVICE

As the United States expanded its territories westward in the early and mid-19th century, Americans ventured out to explore those vast uncharted lands that stretched to the Pacific Ocean. The Lewis and Clark Expedition of 1804–06 and subsequent forays by organized groups and by individuals brought back stories of remarkable wonders that had been seen in the West—places that were later designated as Yellowstone (in Wyoming, Idaho, and Montana), Yosemite (in California's Sierra Nevada), the Grand Canyon (in Arizona), and many others. A growing number of people, notably the naturalist and conservationist John Muir, began calling on the federal government to protect those scenic places from exploitation. In 1871 an expedition to the Yellowstone region led by Ferdinand V. Hayden and sponsored by the U.S. Geological Survey included the photographer William Henry Jackson and the painter Thomas Moran. Upon the expedition's return to the East, Jackson's images of Yellowstone and, especially, a series of spectacular large paintings of the Grand Canyon and other wonders there executed by Moran enthralled the American public. The following year Congress authorized the creation of Yellowstone as the country's—and the world's—first national park.

Congress passed the Antiquities Act of 1906, which gave the president the authority to preserve federal lands by designating them as national monuments. Roosevelt soon proclaimed the first monument, Devils Tower, and over the next 10 years more than 30 other such entities were proclaimed, some half of that total by Roosevelt.

John Muir continued to express concerns that sites of scenic beauty were not being adequately preserved. Muir had the opportunity to state his case directly to U.S. Pres. Theodore Roosevelt—who himself was an avid naturalist and outdoor enthusiast—when the two of them camped together in Yosemite in the summer of 1903.

Yellowstone National Park

Archaeological evidence recovered in Yellowstone indicates that there has been a sustained human presence in the region since sometime after the end of the last glaciation there (about 13,000–14,000 years ago), with the oldest artifacts dating to more than 11,000 years ago. Little is known about those early peoples.

The first person of European ancestry to venture into the Yellowstone region was American trapper and explorer John Colter, who reached the area in 1807–08 after having been a part of and then leaving the Lewis and Clark Expedition in 1806. Other trappers—including Jim Bridger, Joseph Meeks, and Osborne Russell—told of seeing the canyon, lake, and geysers.

Establishment of the National Park Service

By the early 20th century it was clear that a system of national parks was being created in the country. All national parks and most national monuments were under the purview of the Interior Department, but at that time each was administered separately and by different authorities. Yellowstone, for example, was supervised by the U.S. Army. None, however, was being run effectively, in part because few resources were allocated for the parks' operation and maintenance. In addition, in many cases private interests were exploiting resources within the parks by felling timber, grazing livestock, or hunting wildlife.

In 1914 Stephen Mather, a wealthy businessman, wrote the secretary of the interior about the poor condition of parks he had visited that summer in the Sierra Nevada. The secretary suggested that Mather work to improve the system by joining the department in Washington, D.C. Two years later, through the efforts of Mather and his assistant, Horace Albright, Congress passed what was dubbed the "Organic Act," which authorized the formation of the National Park Service (NPS). Mather was named its first director.

Mather and Albright (who succeeded Mather as director in 1929) set out to unify all of the NPS properties under the service's central guidance. They created a corps of NPS superintendents and rangers who brought stability, order, and professionalism to the management of the national parks and monuments. The two men also tirelessly promoted the parks and their wonders, both to encourage more people to visit them and to persuade government authorities to create more parks. More than a dozen new national parks were established between 1916 and 1933 (when Albright stepped down), including Grand Canyon (1919) and (all in May 1926) Great Smoky Mountains, Shenandoah, and Mammoth Cave. Dozens of new national monuments were also named, many of which—including Carlsbad Cave (now Carlsbad Caverns), Glacier Bay, and Death Valley—would later become national parks.

WORLD WAR I

Leading to War and Hoping for Neutrality

The outbreak of general war in Europe in August 1914 raised grave challenges to President Woodrow Wilson's skill and leadership in foreign affairs. In spite of the appeals of propagandists for the rival Allies and Central Powers, the great majority of Americans were doggedly neutral and determined to avoid involvement unless American rights and interests were grossly violated. This, too, was Wilson's own feeling, and in August he issued an official proclamation of neutrality and two weeks later appealed to Americans to be "impartial in thought as well as in action."

There was no possibility of conflict between Germany and the United States so long as the former confined its warfare to the continent of Europe; a new situation full of potential danger arose, however, when the German authorities decided to use their new weapon, the submarine, to challenge British control of the seas.

By the eve of World War I all of the major navies included submarines in their fleets, but these craft were relatively small, were considered of questionable military value, and generally were intended for coastal operations. The most significant exception to the concept of coastal activity was the German Deutschland class of merchant U-boats, each 315 feet long with two large cargo compartments.

The German admiralty announced in February 1915 that all Allied vessels would be torpedoed without warning in a broad area and that even neutral vessels were not safe. Wilson replied at once that he would hold Germany to "strict accountability" (a conventional diplomatic term) if submarines destroyed American ships and lives without warning. The Germans soon gave broad guarantees concerning American ships, and their safety against illegal submarine attacks was not an issue between the two countries before 1917. An issue much more fraught with danger was the safety of Americans traveling and working on Allied ships. A German submarine sank the unarmed British liner *Lusitania* without warning on May 7, 1915, killing, among others, 128 Americans. Wilson at first appealed to the Germans on broad grounds of humanity to abandon submarine warfare, but in the subsequent negotiations he narrowed the issue to one of safety for unarmed passenger liners against violent underseas attack. Momentary resolution came when a submarine sank the unarmed British liner *Arabic* in August. Wilson warned that he would break diplomatic relations if such attacks continued, and the Germans grudgingly promised not to attack unarmed passenger ships without warning. The controversy escalated to a more dangerous level when a submarine torpedoed the packet steamer *Sussex* in the English Channel with heavy loss of life in March 1916. In an ultimatum to Berlin, Wilson threatened to break diplomatic relations if the Germans did not cease attacking liners and merchantmen without warning; once again the Germans capitulated, but they threatened to resume unrestricted submarine warfare if the United States failed to force the British to observe international law in their blockade practices.

The Allies complicated the submarine controversy in late 1915 by arming many of their liners and merchantmen sailing to American ports. Wilson tried to arrange a compromise by which the Allies would disarm their ships in return for a German promise not to sink them without warning. When the British rejected the proposal, the president gave the impression that he would hold Germany accountable for American lives lost on armed ships, setting off a rebellion in Congress and the near passage of resolutions forbidding American citizens to travel on armed ships. Actually, the president had no intention of permitting armed ships to become a serious issue; their status was never a subject of serious controversy between the United States and Germany.

America Readies for War

Meanwhile, the increasingly perilous state of relations with Germany had prompted Wilson, in December 1915, to call for a considerable expansion in the country's armed forces. A violent controversy over preparedness ensued, both in Congress and in the country at large.

On April 22, 1915, the Germans used chlorine gas for the first time on the Western Front, but they made the mistake of discharging it from cylinders (which were dependent on a favorable wind) rather than lobbing it onto the enemy trenches in artillery shells.

Machine guns and rapid-firing artillery, when used in combination with trenches and barbed-wire emplacements, gave a decided advantage to the defense, since these weapons' rapid and sustained firepower could decimate a frontal assault by either infantry or cavalry.

Woodrow Wilson

Wilson's most passionate desire, aside from avoiding belligerency, was to bring an end to the war through his personal mediation. He sent his confidential counselor, Col. Edward M. House of Texas, to Europe in early 1915 to explore the possibilities of peace and again early in 1916 to press for a plan of Anglo-American cooperation for peace. The British refused to cooperate, and the president, eager to avoid a final confrontation with Germany, decided to press forward with independent mediation.

WORLD WAR I

Germany's Submarine Offensive

Chances for peace were blasted by a decision of the German leaders, made at an imperial conference on January 9, 1917, to inaugurate an all-out submarine war against all commerce, neutral as well as belligerent. The Germans knew that such a campaign would bring the United States into the war, but they were confident that their augmented submarine fleet could starve Britain into submission before the United States could mobilize and participate effectively.

The American military contribution was as important as the economic one. There were still only 85,000 U.S. troops in France when the Germans launched their last great offensive in March 1918; but there were 1,200,000 there by the following September.

The announcement of the new submarine blockade in January left the president no alternative but to break diplomatic relations with Germany, which he did on February 3. At the same time, and in subsequent addresses, the president made it clear that he would accept unrestricted submarine warfare against belligerent merchantmen and would act only if American ships were sunk. In early March he put arms on American ships in the hope that this would deter submarine attacks. The Germans began to sink American ships indiscriminately in mid-March, and on April 2 Wilson asked Congress to recognize that a state of war existed between the United States and the German Empire. Congress approved the war resolution quickly, and Wilson signed it on April 6.

The U.S. Navy abandoned its plans for the construction of battleships and instead concentrated on building the destroyers and submarine chasers so desperately needed to protect Allied shipping from the U-boats. By the end of the war there were more than 380 U.S. craft stationed overseas.

America's Contribution to the War

The American military contribution, while small compared to that of the Allies during the entire war, was in two respects decisive in the outcome. The U.S. Navy, fully prepared at the outset, provided the ships that helped the British overcome the submarine threat by the autumn of 1917. The U.S. Army, some 4,000,000 men strong, was raised mainly by conscription under the Selective Service Act of 1917; the American Expeditionary Force of more than 1,200,000 men under General Pershing reached France by September 1918, and this huge infusion of manpower tipped the balance on the Western Front and helped to end the war in November 1918, a year earlier than military planners had anticipated.

Wilson's Fourteen Points

In one of the most ambitious rhetorical efforts in modern history, on Jan. 8, 1918, President Wilson, in his address to the joint session of the United States Congress, formulated under 14 separate heads his ideas of the essential nature for a postwar peace settlement.

In his general points Wilson demanded an end to the old diplomacy that had led to wars in the past. He proposed open diplomacy instead of entangling alliances, and he called for freedom of the seas, an impartial settlement of colonial claims, general disarmament, removal of artificial trade barriers, and, most important, a league of nations to promote peace and protect the territorial integrity and independence of its members. A breathtaking pronouncement, the Fourteen Points gave new hope to millions of liberals and moderate socialists who were fighting for a new international order based upon peace and justice.

With their armies reeling under the weight of a combined Allied and American assault, the Germans appealed to Wilson in October 1918 for an armistice based on the Fourteen Points and other presidential pronouncements.

The Paris Peace Conference and the Versailles Treaty

Wilson led the U.S. delegation and a large group of experts to the peace conference, which opened in Paris in January 1919. He fought heroically for his Fourteen Points against the Allied leaders—David Lloyd George of Britain, Georges Clemenceau of France, and Vittorio Orlando of Italy—who, under heavy pressure from their own constituencies, were determined to divide the territories of the vanquished and make Germany pay the full cost of the war. Wilson made a number of compromises that violated the spirit if not the letter of the Fourteen Points, including the imposition of an indefinitely large reparations bill upon Germany. Moreover, the Allies had intervened in the Russian Civil War against the dominant revolutionary socialist faction, the Bolsheviks, and Wilson had halfheartedly cooperated with the Allies by dispatching small numbers of troops to northern Russia, to protect military supplies against the advancing Germans, and to Siberia, mainly to keep an eye on the Japanese, who had sent a large force there. But Wilson won many more of his Fourteen Points than he lost; his greatest victories were to prevent the dismemberment of Germany in the west and further intervention in Russia and, most important, to obtain the incorporation of the Covenant of the League of Nations into the Versailles Treaty. He was confident that the League, under American leadership, would soon rectify the injustices of the treaty.

Prohibition

In the United States an early wave of movements for state and local prohibition (the legal prevention of the manufacture, sale, and transportation of alcoholic beverages) arose from the intensive religious revivalism of the 1820s and 1830s, which stimulated movements toward perfectionism in human beings, including temperance and abolitionism. The precedent for seeking temperance through law was set by a Massachusetts law, passed in 1838 and repealed two years later, which prohibited sales of spirits in less than 15-gallon (55-litre) quantities. The first state prohibition law was passed in Maine in 1846 and ushered in a wave of such state legislation before the American Civil War.

Most of the organized efforts supporting prohibition involved religious coalitions that linked alcohol to immorality, criminality, and, with the advent of World War I, unpatriotic citizenship.

Conceived by Wayne Wheeler, the leader of the Anti-Saloon League, the Eighteenth Amendment (which imposed the federal prohibition of alcohol) passed in both chambers of the U.S. Congress in December 1917 and was ratified by the requisite three-fourths of the states in January 1919. Its language called for Congress to pass enforcement legislation, and that was championed by Andrew Volstead, chairman of the House Judiciary Committee, who engineered passage of the Volstead Act (which would enforce prohibition) over the veto of Pres. Woodrow Wilson.

Bootlegging and Organized Crime

The earliest bootleggers (those involved in the illegal production and sale of liquor) began smuggling foreign-made commercial liquor into the United States from across the Canadian and Mexican borders and along the seacoasts from ships under foreign registry. That type of smuggling became riskier and more expensive when the U.S. Coast Guard began halting and searching ships at greater distances from the coast and using fast motor launches of its own. Bootleggers had other major sources of supply, however. The distribution of liquor was necessarily more complex than other types of criminal activity, and organized gangs eventually arose that could control an entire local chain of bootlegging operations, from concealed d istilleries and breweries through storage and transport channels to speakeasies, restaurants, nightclubs, and other retail outlets. Those gangs tried to secure and enlarge territories in which they had a monopoly of distribution.

Gradually, the gangs in different cities began to cooperate with each other, and they extended their methods of organizing beyond bootlegging to narcotics traffic, gambling rackets, prostitution, labor racketeering, loan-sharking, and extortion. The American Mafia crime syndicate arose out of the coordinated activities of Italian bootleggers and other gangsters in New York City in the late 1920s and early 1930s.

Neither the Volstead Act nor the Eighteenth Amendment was enforced with great success. Indeed, entire illegal economies (bootlegging, speakeasies, and distilling operations) flourished.

Chicago's Gangsters

Johnny Torrio rose to become a rackets boss in Brooklyn, New York, and then relocated to Chicago, where in the early 1920s he expanded the crime empire founded by James ("Big Jim") Colosimo into big-time bootlegging. Torrio turned over his rackets in 1925 to Al Capone, who became the Prohibition era's most famous gangster, though other crime czars such as Dion O'Bannion (Capone's rival in Chicago), Joe Masseria, Meyer Lansky, Lucky Luciano, and Bugsy Siegel were also legendarily infamous. Capone's wealth in 1927 was estimated at close to $100 million.

In 1929—the year of the stock market crash, which seemingly increased the country's desire for illegal liquor—Eliot Ness was hired as a special agent of the U.S. Department of Justice to head the Prohibition bureau in Chicago, with the express purpose of investigating and harassing Capone. Because the men whom Ness hired to help him were extremely dedicated and unbribable, they were nicknamed the Untouchables. The public learned of them when big raids on breweries, speakeasies, and other places of outlawry attracted newspaper headlines. The Untouchables' infiltration of the underworld secured evidence that helped send Capone to prison for income-tax evasion in 1932.

St. Valentine's Day Massacre

The St. Valentine's Day Massacre was a bloody incident that dramatized the intense rivalry for control of the illegal liquor traffic during the Prohibition Era in the United States. In 1929, disguising themselves as policemen, members of the Al Capone gang entered a garage at 2122 North Clark Street run by members of the George "Bugs" Moran gang, lined their opponents up against a wall, and shot them in cold blood. The St. Valentine's Day Massacre and other gangland killings, frequently portrayed vividly by the mass media throughout the world, came to symbolize the violence of the Prohibition Era in Chicago.

The Great Depression

The worldwide economic downturn known as the Great Depression began in the U.S. as a recession in 1929. The downturn became markedly worse, however, in late 1929 and continued until early 1933. Real output and prices fell precipitously. Between the peak and the trough of the downturn, industrial production in the United States declined 47 percent and real gross domestic product (GDP) fell 30 percent. The wholesale price index declined 33 percent (such declines in the price level are referred to as deflation). Although there is some debate about the reliability of the statistics, it is widely agreed that the unemployment rate exceeded 20 percent at its highest point. The severity of the Great Depression in the United States becomes especially clear when it is compared with America's next worst recession of the 20th century, that of 1981–82, when the country's real GDP declined just 2 percent and the unemployment rate peaked at less than 10 percent. Moreover, during the 1981–82 recession prices continued to rise, although the rate of price increase slowed substantially (a phenomenon known as disinflation).

The Depression affected virtually every country of the world. However, the dates and magnitude of the downturn varied substantially across countries.

The Causes

The initial decline in U.S. output in the summer of 1929 is widely believed to have stemmed from tight U.S. monetary policy aimed at limiting stock market speculation. The 1920s had been a prosperous decade, but not an exceptional boom period; prices had remained nearly constant throughout the decade, and there had been mild recessions in both 1924 and 1927. The one obvious area of excess was the stock market. Stock prices had risen more than fourfold from the low in 1921 to the peak in 1929. In 1928 and 1929, the Federal Reserve had raised interest rates in hopes of slowing the rapid rise in stock prices. These higher interest rates depressed interest-sensitive spending in areas such as construction and automobile purchases, which in turn reduced production. Some scholars believe that a boom in housing construction in the mid-1920s led to an excess supply of housing and a particularly large drop in construction in 1928 and 1929.

By the fall of 1929, U.S. stock prices had reached levels that could not be justified by reasonable anticipations of future earnings. As a result, when a variety of minor events led to gradual price

The most devastating impact of the Great Depression was human suffering. In a short period of time, world output and standards of living dropped precipitously.

declines in October 1929, investors lost confidence and the stock market bubble burst. Panic selling began on "Black Thursday," October 24, 1929.

The next blow to aggregate demand occurred in the fall of 1930, when the first of four waves of banking panics gripped the United States. A banking panic arises when many depositors simultaneously lose confidence in the solvency of banks and demand that their bank deposits be paid to them in cash. Banks, which typically hold only a fraction of deposits as cash reserves, must liquidate loans in order to raise the required cash. This process of hasty liquidation can cause even a previously solvent bank to fail.

The Effects

The Great Depression and the policy response changed the world economy in crucial ways. Most obviously, it hastened, if not caused, the end of the international gold standard. Although a system of fixed currency exchange rates was reinstated after World War II under the Bretton Woods system, the economies of the world never embraced that system with the conviction and fervour they had brought to the gold standard.

As much as one-fourth of the labor force in industrialized countries was unable to find work in the early 1930s. While conditions began to improve by the mid-1930s, total recovery was not accomplished until the end of the decade.

Both labor unions and the welfare state expanded substantially during the 1930s. In the United States, union membership more than doubled between 1930 and 1940. This trend was stimulated by both the severe unemployment of the 1930s and the passage of the National Labor Relations (Wagner) Act (1935), which encouraged collective bargaining. The United States also established unemployment compensation and old-age and survivors' insurance through the Social Security Act (1935), which was passed in response to the hardships of the 1930s. It is uncertain whether these changes would have eventually occurred in the United States without the Great Depression. Many European countries had experienced significant increases in union membership and had established government pensions before the 1930s. Both of these trends, however, accelerated in Europe during the Great Depression.

The Great Depression

Given the key roles of monetary contraction and the gold standard in causing the Great Depression, it is not surprising that currency devaluations and monetary expansion were the leading sources of recovery throughout the world. There is a notable correlation between the times at which countries abandoned the gold standard (or devalued their currencies substantially) and when they experienced renewed growth in their output. For example, Britain, which was forced off the gold standard in September 1931, recovered relatively early, while the United States, which did not effectively devalue its currency until 1933, recovered substantially later.

Devaluation, however, did not increase output directly. Rather, it allowed countries to expand their money supplies without concern about gold movements and exchange rates. Countries that took greater advantage of this freedom saw greater recovery. The monetary expansion that began in the United States in early 1933 was particularly dramatic. The American money supply increased nearly 42 percent between 1933 and 1937. This monetary expansion stemmed largely from a substantial gold inflow to the United States, caused in part by the rising political tensions in Europe that eventually led to World War II. Monetary expansion stimulated spending by lowering interest rates and making credit more widely available. It also created expectations of inflation, rather than deflation, thereby giving potential borrowers greater confidence that their wages and profits would be sufficient to cover their loan payments if they chose to borrow. One sign that monetary expansion stimulated recovery in the United States by encouraging borrowing was that consumer and business spending on interest-sensitive items such as cars, trucks, and machinery rose well before consumer spending on services.

The worst drought in modern American history struck the Great Plains in 1934. Windstorms that stripped the topsoil from millions of acres turned the whole area into a vast Dust Bowl and destroyed crops and livestock in unprecedented amounts. As a result, some 2.5 million people fled the Plains states, many bound for California, where the promise of sunshine and a better life often collided with the reality of scarce, poorly paid work as migrant farm laborers.

The New Deal

The New Deal was the domestic economic relief program of President Franklin D. Roosevelt that generally embraced the concept of a government-regulated economy aimed at achieving a balance between conflicting economic interests. Much of the New Deal legislation was enacted within the first three months of Franklin D. Roosevelt's presidency, which became known as the

Hundred Days. The new administration's first objective was to alleviate the suffering of the nation's huge number of unemployed workers. Such agencies as the Works Progress Administration (WPA) and the Civilian Conservation Corps (CCC) were established to dispense emergency and short-term governmental aid and to provide temporary jobs, employment on construction projects, and youth work in the national forests. Before 1935 the New Deal focused on revitalizing the country's stricken business and agricultural communities. To revive industrial activity, the National Recovery Administration (NRA) was granted authority to help shape industrial codes governing trade practices, wages, hours, child labor, and collective bargaining. The New Deal also tried to regulate the nation's financial hierarchy in order to avoid a repetition of the stock market crash of 1929 and the massive bank failures that followed. The Federal Deposit Insurance Corporation (FDIC) granted government insurance for bank deposits in member banks of the Federal Reserve System, and the Securities and Exchange Commission (SEC) was formed to protect the investing public from fraudulent stock-market practices. The farm program was centered in the Agricultural Adjustment Administration (AAA), which attempted to raise prices by controlling the production of staple crops through cash subsidies to farmers. In addition, the arm of the federal government reached into the area of electric power, establishing in 1933 the Tennessee Valley Authority (TVA), which was to cover a seven-state area and supply cheap electricity, prevent floods, improve navigation, and produce nitrates.

For Americans, the 1930s will always summon up images of breadlines, apple sellers on street corners, shuttered factories, rural poverty, and so-called Hoovervilles (named for President Herbert Hoover), where homeless families sought refuge in shelters cobbled together from salvaged wood, cardboard, and tin.

No matter how insular Americans were through much of the decade, the world arrived on their shores in the 1930s. At the moment that Americans were worrying about their economy, European intellectuals, scientists, scholars, artists, and filmmakers were literally running for their lives. Where a lot of them ran was to the United States.

WORLD WAR II:
Europe and Asia Go to War

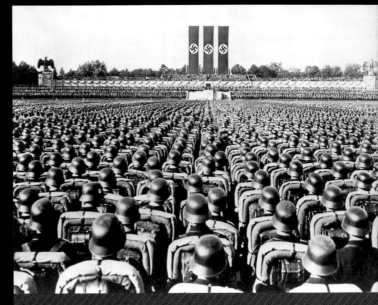

In September 1939 the Allies, namely Great Britain, France, and Poland, were together superior in industrial resources, population, and military manpower, but the German Army, or Wehrmacht, because of its armament, training, doctrine, discipline, and fighting spirit, was the most efficient and effective fighting force for its size in the world.

Japan Invades China

Overt hostilities between Japan and China began after the Marco Polo Bridge incident of July 7, 1937, when shots were exchanged between Chinese and Japanese troops on the outskirts of Peking. Open fighting broke out in that area, and in late July the Japanese

The Japanese needed large numbers of troops to maintain their hold on the immense Chinese territories and populations they controlled. Of the 51 infantry divisions making up the Japanese Army in 1941, 38 of them, comprising about 750,000 men, were stationed in China.

captured the Peking-Tientsin area. Thereupon full-scale hostilities began between the two nations. The Japanese landed near Shanghai, at the mouth of the Yangtze River, and took Shanghai in November and the Chinese capital, Nanking, in December 1937.

Nationalist Chinese resistance to these Japanese advances was ineffective, primarily because the Nationalist leadership was still more interested in holding their forces in reserve for a future struggle with the Communists than in repelling the Japanese.

German Strategy

German strategy in World War II is wholly intelligible only if Hitler's far-reaching system of power politics and his racist ideology are borne in mind. Since the 1920s his program had been first to win power in Germany proper, next to consolidate Germany's domination over Central Europe, and then to raise Germany to the status of a world power by two stages: (1) the building up of a continental empire embracing all Europe, including the European portion of the Soviet Union, and (2) the attainment for Germany of equal rank with the British Empire, Japan, and the United States—the only world powers to be left after the elimination of France and the U.S.S.R.

The conquest of the European part of the Soviet Union, which in Hitler's calendar was dated approximately for 1943–45, was to be preceded, he thought, by short localized campaigns elsewhere in Europe to provide a strategic shield and to secure Germany's rear for the great expedition of conquest in the East, which was also bound up with the extermination of the Jews. The most important of the localized campaigns would be that against France. But Hitler became acutely suspicious of the intentions of the Soviet leader, Joseph Stalin, and he began to feel that he could not afford to wait to complete the subjugation of western Europe before dealing with the Soviet Union.

The Holocaust

Even before the Nazis came to power in Germany in 1933, they had made no secret of their anti-Semitism. Nazi anti-Semitism was rooted in religious anti-Semitism and enhanced by political anti-Semitism. To this the Nazis added a further dimension: racial anti-Semitism. Ultimately, the logic of Nazi racial anti-Semitism led to annihilation.

In early 1942 the Nazis built their first extermination camps. The death camps were to be the essential instrument of the "final solution." The extermination camps became factories producing corpses, effectively and efficiently, at minimal physical and psychological cost to German personnel. The intensity of the Nazi campaign against the Jews continued unabated to the very end of the war and at points even took priority over German military efforts. Upon liberating the camps, many Allied units were so shocked by what they saw that they meted out spontaneous punishment to some of the remaining camp personnel. Others were arrested and held for trial. In all, some six million Jewish men, women, and children and millions of others were exterminated by Nazi Germany and its collaborators during the war.

WORLD WAR II:
America Goes to War

Eventually more than 15,000,000 men and women would serve in the armed forces, but not until 1943 would the United States be strong enough to undertake large-scale offensive operations.

After World War I most Americans concluded that participating in international affairs had been a mistake. They sought peace through isolation and throughout the 1920s advocated a policy of disarmament and nonintervention. As the European situation became more tense, the United States continued to hold to its isolationist policy.

In the Pacific, President Roosevelt continued Herbert Hoover's policy of non-recognition of Japan's conquests in Asia. When Japan invaded China in 1937, however, he seemed to begin moving away from isolationism. He did not invoke the Neutrality Act, which had just been revised, and in October he warned that war was like a disease and suggested that it might be desirable for peace-loving nations to "quarantine" aggressor nations. When Germany's invasion of Poland in 1939 touched off World War II, Roosevelt called Congress into special session to revise the Neutrality Act to allow belligerents (in reality only Great Britain and France, both on the Allied side) to purchase munitions on a cash-and-carry basis. With the fall of France to Germany in June 1940, Roosevelt, with heavy public support, threw the resources of the United States behind the British.

The war question was soon resolved by events in the Pacific. As much as a distant neutral could, the United States had been supporting China in its war against Japan, yet it continued to sell Japan products and commodities essential to the Japanese war effort. Then, in July 1940, the United States applied an embargo on the sale of aviation gas, lubricants, and prime scrap metal to Japan. When Japanese armies invaded French Indochina in September with the apparent purpose of establishing bases for an attack on the East Indies, the United States struck back by embargoing all types of scrap iron and steel and by extending a loan to China. Japan promptly retaliated by signing a limited treaty of alliance, the Tripartite Pact, with Germany and Italy. Japan and the United States then entered into complex negotiations in the spring of 1941. Neither country would compromise on the China question, however, Japan refusing to withdraw and the United States insisting upon it. Believing that Japan intended to attack the East Indies the United States stopped exporting oil to Japan at the end of the summer. In effect an ultimatum, since Japan had limited oil stocks and no alternative source of supply, the oil embargo confirmed Japan's decision to eliminate the U.S. Pacific Fleet and to conquer Southeast Asia, thereby becoming self-sufficient in crude oil and other vital resources.

On December 7, 1941, Japan directed its first blow against naval and air installations in Hawaii. In a bold surprise attack, Japanese aircraft destroyed or damaged 18 ships of war at Pearl Harbor, including the entire battleship force, and 347 planes. Total U.S. casualties amounted to 2,403 dead and 1,178 wounded.

On December 8 Congress with only one dissenting vote declared war against Japan. Three days later Germany and Italy declared war against the United States; and Congress, voting unanimously, reciprocated. As a result of the attack on Pearl Harbor, the previously divided nation entered into the global struggle with virtual unanimity.

Social Consequences at Home

Because the attack on Pearl Harbor had united the nation behind joining the war, few people were prosecuted for disloyalty or sedition, unlike during World War I. The one glaring exception to this policy was the scandalous treatment of Japanese and Americans of Japanese descent. In 1942, on the basis of groundless racial fears and suspicions, virtually the entire Japanese-American population of the West Coast, amounting to 110,000 persons, was rounded up and imprisoned in "relocation" centers, which the inmates regarded as concentration camps. The Japanese-Americans lost their liberty, and in most cases their property as well, despite the fact that the Federal Bureau of Investigation, which had already arrested those individuals it considered security risks, had verified their loyalty.

The United States dropped atomic bombs on the Japanese cities of Hiroshima (August 6, 1945) and Nagasaki (August 9). The first bombs devastated the heart of Hiroshima, killing 70,000 immediately. The terrain and smaller size of Nagasaki reduced the destruction of life and property, but 39,000 persons were killed and 25,000 were injured. The Japanese initiated surrender negotiations the next day.

There can be no real statistical measurement of the human and material cost of World War II. The money cost to governments involved has been estimated at more than $1,000,000,000,000 but this figure cannot represent the human misery, deprivation, and suffering, the dislocation of peoples and of economic life, or the sheer physical destruction of property that the war involved.

The Formation of the CIA

The United States was the last of the major powers to establish a civilian intelligence agency responsible for the collection of secret information for policy makers. Indeed, prior to 1942 the country lacked any civilian intelligence agency. Information was collected in an unsystematic way by the Office of Naval Intelligence, by U.S. Army intelligence, and by the FBI. The information gathered was rarely shared with other government agencies and was sometimes not even provided to senior policy makers. For example, because of rivalries between army and navy intelligence offices, which did not want to jeopardize the "security" of their information, President Franklin D. Roosevelt was not given sensitive information about Japan in the months before the Japanese attacked Pearl Harbor in December 1941.

In the early days of the Cold War, the CIA and the U.S. military intelligence services smuggled former Nazi intelligence officers out of Europe, and the agency worked with several former Nazis to conduct intelligence operations in eastern Europe and the Soviet Union.

In June 1942 Roosevelt created the Office of Stategic Services (OSS) to bring together the fragmented and uncoordinated strands of U.S. foreign intelligence gathering in a single organization. During World War II the OSS, with a staff of approximately 12,000, collected and analyzed information on areas of the world in which U.S. military forces were operating. It used agents inside Nazi-occupied Europe, including Berlin; carried out counterpropaganda and disinformation activities; produced analytical reports for policy makers; and staged special operations (e.g., sabotage and demolition) behind enemy lines to support guerrillas and resistance fighters. Before the Allied invasion of Normandy in June 1944, more than 500 OSS agents were working inside occupied France. Among reports commissioned from the OSS were assessments of German industry and war-making capability and a psychological profile of German dictator Adolf Hitler that concluded that he would likely commit suicide should Germany be defeated.

In 1946 President Harry S. Truman, recognizing the need for a coordinated postwar intelligence establishment, created by executive order a Central Intelligence Group and a National Intelligence Authority, both of which recruited key former members of the OSS. As in the days of the OSS, there were problems of distrust and rivalry between the new civilian agencies and the military intelligence services and the FBI.

In 1947 Congress passed the National Security Act, which created the National Security Council (NSC) and, under its direction, the Central Intelligence Agency (CIA). Given extensive power to conduct foreign intelligence operations, the CIA was charged with advising the NSC on intelligence matters, correlating and evaluating the intelligence activities of other government agencies, and carrying out other intelligence activities as the NSC might require. Although it did not end rivalries with the military services and the FBI, the law established the CIA as the country's preeminent intelligence service. The agency was popularly thought of as the U.S. counterpart of the Soviet KGB, though, unlike the KGB, the CIA was forbidden by law (the National Security Act) from conducting intelligence and counterintelligence operations on domestic soil. In contrast, the majority of the KGB's operations took place within the Soviet Union and against Soviet citizens.

Activities

The publication of post-Cold War memoirs by former agents and the release of declassified documents by the United States and Russia have provided a fairly complete account of the CIA's activities, including both its successes and its failures. CIA data collection and analysis was important for arms-control negotiations with the Soviet Union throughout the Cold War and for determining U.S. strategy during the 1962 Cuban Missile Crisis, when President John F. Kennedy relied on information gathered by the CIA through Soviet double agent Colonel Oleg Penkovsky. During the 1970s and 1980s, CIA agents in the Soviet military and the KGB provided information on the Soviet military-industrial complex. During the Cold War, CIA technical operations included the bugging of the Soviet military's major communications line in East Germany and the development of reconnaissance aircraft

The CIA was unsuccessful in its multiple attempts to assassinate Cuban leader Fidel Castro in the 1960s.

such as the U-2 and spy satellites capable of photographing targets as small as a rocket silo. Aerial reconnaissance—first by plane and then by satellite—provided early warning of the deployment of Soviet missiles in Cuba and the development of new missiles in the Soviet Union.

Criticism

The CIA has been criticized for conducting covert actions that some consider immoral or illegal under international law, for maintaining close ties to human rights abusers and other criminals, for failing to safeguard its own operations, and, from 2001, for kidnapping, torturing, and illegally detaining foreign nationals. The CIA often has been portrayed by its critics as an agency run amok that implements covert operations without the approval of the executive branch of the U.S. government. Contrary to that assertion, however, all covert operations must be officially sanctioned by the executive branch. Once approved by the National Security Council, plans for covert action are presented to the Senate and House committees that oversee CIA operations.

From 2001, critics of the CIA's campaign against al-Qaeda argued that many of the activities it encompassed, in particular the use of enhanced interrogation techniques, were unconstitutional or illegal under U.S. and international law.

The North Atlantic TREATY ORGANIZATION

After World War II in 1945, western Europe was economically exhausted and militarily weak (the western Allies had rapidly and drastically reduced their armies at the end of the war), and newly powerful communist parties had arisen in France and Italy. By contrast, the Soviet Union had emerged from the war with its armies dominating all the states of central and eastern Europe, and by 1948 communists under Moscow's sponsorship had consolidated their control of the governments of those countries and suppressed all noncommunist political activity. The Iron Curtain, a term popularized by British statesman Winston Churchill, had descended upon central and eastern Europe. Further, wartime cooperation between the western Allies and the Soviets had completely broken down. Each side was organizing its own sector of occupied Germany, so that two German states would emerge, a democratic one in the west and a communist one in the east.

In 1948 the United States launched the Marshall Plan, which infused massive amounts of economic aid to the countries of western and southern Europe on the condition that they cooperate with each other and engage in joint planning to hasten their mutual recovery. As for military recovery, under the Brussels Treaty of 1948, the United Kingdom, France, and the Low Countries—Belgium, the Netherlands, and Luxembourg—concluded a collective-defense agreement called the Western European Union. It was soon recognized, however, that a more formidable alliance would be required to provide an adequate military counterweight to the Soviets.

By this time Britain, Canada, and the United States had already engaged in secret exploratory talks on security arrangements that would serve as an alternative to the United Nations (UN), which was becoming paralyzed by the rapidly emerging Cold War. In March 1948, following a virtual communist *coup d'état* in Czechoslovakia in February, the three governments began discussions on a multilateral collective-defense scheme that would enhance Western security and promote democratic values. These discussions were eventually joined by France, the Low Countries, and Norway and in April 1949 resulted in the North Atlantic Treaty.

The Iron Curtain was a political, military, and ideological barrier erected by the Soviet Union after World War II to seal off itself and its dependent eastern and central European allies from open contact with the West and other noncommunist areas.

Organization

Spurred by the North Korean invasion of South Korea in June 1950, the United States took steps to demonstrate that it would resist any Soviet military expansion or pressures in Europe.

A serious issue confronting NATO in the early and mid-1950s was the negotiation of West Germany's participation in the alliance. The prospect of a rearmed Germany was understandably greeted with widespread unease and hesitancy in western Europe, but the country's strength had long been recognized as necessary to protect western Europe from a possible Soviet invasion.

General Dwight D. Eisenhower, the leader of the Allied forces in western Europe in World War II, was named Supreme Allied Commander Europe (SACEUR) by the North Atlantic Council (NATO's governing body) in December 1950. He was followed as SACEUR by a succession of American generals. NATO's military organization encompasses a complete system of commands for possible wartime use. During the alliance's first 20 years, more than $3 billion worth of "infrastructure" for NATO forces—bases, airfields, pipelines, communications networks, depots—was jointly planned, financed, and built, with about one-third of the funding from the United States. NATO funding generally is not used for the procurement of military equipment, which is provided by the member states—though the NATO Airborne Early Warning Force, a fleet of radar-bearing aircraft designed to protect against a surprise low-flying attack, was funded jointly.

NATO During the Cold War

From its founding, NATO's primary purpose was to unify and strengthen the Western Allies' military response to a possible invasion of western Europe by the Soviet Union, Albania, Bulgaria, Hungary, Poland and other members of the mutal-defense organization known as the Warsaw Pact (May 14, 1955–July 1, 1991). In the early 1950s NATO relied partly on the threat of massive nuclear retaliation from the United States to counter the Warsaw Pact's much larger ground forces. Beginning in 1957, this policy was supplemented by the deployment of American nuclear weapons in western European bases. NATO later adopted a "flexible response" strategy, which the United States interpreted to mean that a war in Europe did not have to escalate to an all-out nuclear exchange. Under this strategy, many Allied forces were equipped with American battlefield and theater nuclear weapons under a dual-control (or "dual-key") system, which allowed both the country hosting the weapons and the United States to veto their use.

From 1961 to 1989 the Brandenburg Gate came to symbolize divided Germany, as the Berlin Wall shut off access to the gate for both East and West Germans. The gate was reopened on December 22, 1989, in the course of the reunification of East and West Berlin.

THE COLD WAR

Following the surrender of Nazi Germany in May 1945 near the close of World War II, the uneasy wartime alliance between the United States and Great Britain on the one hand and the Soviet Union on the other began to unravel. By 1948 the Soviets had installed left-wing governments in the countries of eastern Europe that had been liberated by the Red Army. The Americans and the British feared the permanent Soviet domination of eastern Europe and the threat of Soviet-influenced communist parties coming to power in the democracies of western Europe. The Soviets, on the other hand, were determined to maintain control of eastern Europe in order to safeguard against any possible renewed threat from Germany, and they were intent on spreading communism worldwide, largely for ideological reasons. The Cold War had solidified by 1947–48, when U.S. aid provided under the Marshall Plan to western Europe had brought those countries under American influence and the Soviets had installed openly communist regimes in eastern Europe.

The term "Cold War" was first used by the English writer George Orwell in an article published in 1945 to refer to what he predicted would be a nuclear stalemate between "two or three monstrous super-states, each possessed of a weapon by which millions of people can be wiped out in a few seconds."

The Struggle Between Superpowers

The Cold War reached its peak in 1948–53. In this period the Soviets unsuccessfully blockaded the Western-held sectors of West Berlin (1948–49); the United States and its European allies formed the North Atlantic Treaty Organization (NATO), a unified military command to resist the Soviet presence in Europe (1949); the Soviets exploded their first atomic warhead (1949), thus ending the American monopoly on the atomic bomb; the Chinese communists came to power in mainland China (1949); and the Soviet-supported communist government of North Korea invaded U.S.-supported South Korea in 1950, setting off an indecisive Korean War that lasted until 1953.

From 1953 to 1957 Cold War tensions relaxed somewhat, largely owing to the death of the longtime Soviet dictator Joseph Stalin in 1953; nevertheless, the standoff remained. A unified military organization among the Soviet-bloc countries, the Warsaw Pact, was formed in 1955; and West Germany was admitted into NATO that same year. Another intense stage of the Cold War was in 1958–62. The United States and the Soviet Union began developing intercontinental ballistic missiles, and in 1962 the Soviets began secretly installing missiles in Cuba that could be used to launch nuclear attacks on U.S. cities. This sparked the Cuban Missile Crisis (1962), a confrontation that brought the two superpowers to the brink of war before an agreement was reached to withdraw the missiles.

The Red Scare

Harry Truman's last years in office were marred by charges that his administration was lax about, or even condoned, subversion and disloyalty and that communists, called "reds," had infiltrated the government. These accusations were made despite Truman's strongly anticommunist foreign policy and his creation, in 1947, of an elaborate Federal Employee Loyalty Program, which resulted in hundreds of federal workers being fired and in several thousand more being forced to resign.

The excessive fear of communist subversion was fed by numerous sources. China's fall to communism and the announcement of a Soviet atomic explosion in 1949 alarmed many, and fighting between communist and U.S.-supported factions in Korea heightened political emotions as well.

Real cases of disloyalty and espionage also contributed to the Red Scare, notably the theft of atomic secrets, for which Soviet agent Julius Rosenberg and his wife, Ethel, were convicted in 1951 and executed two years later. Republican Party politicians had much to gain from exploiting these and related issues.

Throughout the Cold War the United States and the Soviet Union avoided direct military confrontation in Europe and engaged in actual combat operations only to keep allies from defecting to the other side or to overthrow them after they had done so.

THE KOREAN WAR

The Korean War had its immediate origins in the collapse of the Japanese empire at the end of World War II in September 1945. Korea, annexed to Japan since 1910, did not have a native government waiting to return after hostilities ceased.

In their hurried effort to disarm the Japanese army and repatriate the Japanese population in Korea (estimated at 700,000), the United States and the Soviet Union agreed in August 1945 to divide the country for administrative purposes at the 38th parallel (latitude 38° N). At least from the American perspective, this geographic division was a temporary expedient; however, the Soviets began a short-lived reign of terror in northern Korea that quickly politicized the division by driving thousands of refugees south. The two sides could not agree on a formula that would produce a unified Korea, and in 1947 U.S. President Harry S. Truman persuaded the United Nations (UN) to assume responsibility for the country, though the U.S. military remained nominally in control of the South until 1948. Both the South Korean national police and the constabulary doubled in size, providing a southern security force of about 80,000 by 1947. In the meantime, Kim Il-sung strengthened his control over the Communist Party as well as the North's administrative structure and military forces. In 1948 the North Korean military and police numbered about 100,000, reinforced by a group of southern Korean guerrillas based at Haeju in western Korea.

The creation of an independent South Korea became UN policy in early 1948. Southern communists opposed this, and by autumn partisan warfare had engulfed parts of every Korean province below the 38th parallel. The fighting expanded into a limited border war between the South's newly formed Republic of Korea Army (ROKA) and the North Korean border constabulary as well as the North's Korean People's Army (KPA). The North launched 10 cross-border guerrilla incursions in order to draw ROKA units away from their guerrilla-suppression campaign in the South.

The Invasion

In the predawn hours of June 25, 1950, the North Koreans struck across the 38th parallel behind a thunderous artillery barrage. The principal offensive drove across the Imjin River toward Seoul. The second offense attacked along two widely separated axes, one through the cities of Chuncheon and Inje to Hongcheon and the other down the east coast road toward Gangneung. The KPA entered Seoul in the afternoon of June 28, but the North Koreans did not accomplish their goal of a quick surrender by the southern government and the disintegration of the South Korean army. Instead, remnants of the Seoul-area ROKA forces formed a defensive line south of the Han River, and on the east coast road ROKA units gave ground in good order. Still, if the South was to stave off collapse, it would need help—from the U.S. armed forces. Under U.S. guidance, the UN called for the invasion to halt (June 25), then for the UN member states to provide military assistance to the ROK. Congressional and public opinion in the United States supported military intervention without significant dissent.

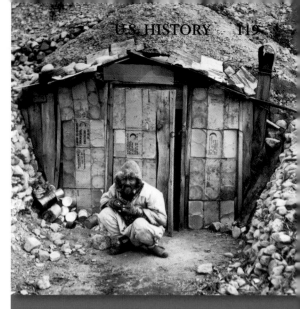

After more than a million combat casualties had been suffered on both sides, the fighting ended in July 1953 with Korea still divided into two hostile states. Negotiations in 1954 produced no further agreement, and the front line has been accepted ever since as the de facto boundary between North and South Korea.

The Truman administration faced the unhappy truth that it did not have much effective military power to meet the invasion. General MacArthur secured the commitment of three divisions from Japan, but U.S. ground forces only expanded the scope of defeat.

Negotiations, Stalemate, and Armistice

By June 1951 the Korean War had reached a critical point. The Chinese–North Korean armies, despite having suffered some 500,000 casualties since November, had grown to 1,200,000 soldiers. United Nations Command had taken its share of casualties—more than 100,000 since the Chinese intervention. These developments obliged the leaders of both coalitions to consider that peace could not be imposed by either side through military victory —at least at acceptable cost. From the time the liaison officers of both coalitions met on July 8, 1951, until the armistice agreement was signed on July 27, 1953, the Korean War continued as a "stalemate." Peace was not yet at hand, however. The South's government had never publicly surrendered their "march north and unify" position, and in private they hinted that they might "accept" an armistice only in return for serious commitments by the United States, including an unambiguous mutual security alliance and economic aid. The Chinese, meanwhile, saw but one way to win concessions and territory in a peace agreement: on the battlefield. The Chinese ordered further attacks on the ROKA. The Americans shared their fury but, in the interest of compromise, convinced the South that the United States would meet all their preconditions for an armistice.

Peace, Growth, Prosperity

The stalemated Korean War, a renewal of inflation, and the continuing Red Scare persuaded President Truman not to stand for reelection in 1952 and also gravely handicapped Gov. Adlai E. Stevenson of Illinois, the Democratic nominee. His opponent, Gen. Dwight D. Eisenhower, was an immensely popular war hero with great personal charm and no political record, making him extremely hard to attack. Although he disliked their methods, Eisenhower allowed Republican campaigners, including his running mate, Sen. Richard M. Nixon of California, to capitalize on the Red Scare by accusing the Truman administration of disloyalty. Eisenhower himself charged the administration with responsibility for the communist invasion of Korea and won wide acclaim when he dramatically promised that if elected he would visit Korea in person to end the war.

Eisenhower won over many farmers, ethnic whites, workers, and Roman Catholics who had previously voted Democratic. Because the Republican margin was slight, and because many right-wing Republicans in Congress disagreed with his policies, Eisenhower would increasingly depend upon Democrats to realize his objectives.

Eisenhower had promised to end the Korean War, hold the line on government spending, balance the budget, abolish inflation, and reform the Republican Party.

Eisenhower Fullfills His Promises

On July 27, 1953, an armistice was signed in Korea freezing the status quo. By cutting defense spending while taxes remained fairly high, and by keeping a tight rein on credit, Eisenhower was able to avoid serious deficits, abolish inflation, and, despite several small recessions, encourage steady economic growth that made Americans more prosperous than they had ever been before. Eisenhower also supported public works and a modest expansion of government social programs. In 1954 the St. Lawrence Seaway Development

As for military policy, Eisenhower instituted the "New Look," which entailed reducing the army from 1,500,000 men in 1953 to 900,000 in 1960. The navy experienced smaller reductions, while air force expenditures rose. Eisenhower was primarily interested in deterring a nuclear attack and to that end promoted expensive developments in nuclear weaponry and long-range missiles.

Corporation was established by Congress. In 1956 Congress authorized the National System of Interstate and Defense Highways, Eisenhower's pet project and the largest public works program in history. Amendments to the Social Security Act in 1954 and 1956 extended benefits to millions not previously covered. Tensions eased in foreign affairs as well. On March 5, 1953, Joseph Stalin died, opening the door to better relations with the Soviet Union. In 1955 the Soviets agreed to end the four-power occupation of Austria, and in that July Eisenhower met in Geneva with the new Soviet leader, Nikita S. Khrushchev, for talks that were friendly though inconclusive. In short, Eisenhower was so successful in restoring tranquillity that, by the end of his first term, some people were complaining that life had become too dull.

Domestic Issues

Although the Eisenhower administration can, in general, be characterized as a period of growth and prosperity, some problems did begin to arise during the second term. In 1957–58 an economic recession hit and unemployment rose to its highest level since 1941. Labor problems increased in intensity, with some 500,000 steelworkers going on strike for 116 days in 1959. There was even evidence of corruption on the Eisenhower staff. The president remained personally popular, but public discontent was demonstrated in the large majorities gained by the Democrats in the congressional elections of 1958.

During Eisenhower's second term, race became a central national concern for the first time since Reconstruction. Some civil rights advances had been made in previous years. In 1954 the Supreme Court had ruled that racially segregated schools were unconstitutional. The decision provoked intense resistance in the South but was followed by a chain of rulings and orders that continually narrowed the right to discriminate. In 1955 Martin Luther King, Jr., led a boycott of segregated buses in Montgomery, Alabama, giving rise to the nonviolent civil rights movement. But neither the president nor Congress became involved in the race issue until 1957, when the segregationist governor of Arkansas blocked the integration of a high school in Little Rock.

The U.S. population, which had grown markedly throughout the 1950s, passed 179 million in 1960. Growth was concentrated in the West, and the country became increasingly urbanized as the middle class moved from the cities to new suburban developments. The migration left cities without their tax base but with responsibility for an increasing number of poor residents. It also resulted in a huge increase in commuters, which in turn led to continuing problems of traffic and pollution.

The Founding of NASA

The National Aeronautics and Space Administration (NASA) was created largely in response to the Soviet launching of Sputnik, the world's first artificial Earth satellite, in 1957. It was organized around the National Advisory Committee for Aeronautics (NACA), which had been created by Congress in 1915. NASA's organization was well underway by the early years of President John F. Kennedy's administration (1961–63), when Kennedy proposed that the United States put a man on the Moon by the end of the 1960s. To that end the Apollo program was designed. Later unmanned programs—such as Viking, Mariner, Voyager, and Galileo—explored other bodies of the solar system. NASA was also responsible for the development and launching of a number of satellites with Earth applications, such as Landsat, a series of satellites designed to collect information on natural resources and other Earth features; communications satellites; and weather satellites. It also planned and developed the space shuttle, a reusable vehicle capable of carrying out missions that could not be conducted with conventional spacecraft.

Apollo 11, in July 1969, climaxed the step-by-step procedure with a lunar landing; on July 20 astronaut Neil Armstrong became the first human to set foot on the Moon's surface.

NASA's Organization

NASA is composed of five program offices: Aeronautics and Space Technology, for the development of equipment; Space Science and Applications, dealing with programs for understanding the origin, structure, and evolution of the universe, the solar system, and the Earth; Space Flight, concerning manned and unmanned space transportation and all matters to do with the space shuttle; Space Tracking and Data, involving tracking and data acquisition; and Space Station, which has a long-term goal of

Apollo missions carried out extensive exploration of the lunar surface, collecting 382 kg (842 pounds) of Moon rocks and installing many instruments for scientific research, such as the solar wind experiment, and the seismographic measurements of the lunar surface.

establishing a manned space station. A number of additional research centers are affiliated, including the Goddard Space Flight Center in Greenbelt, Maryland; the Jet Propulsion Laboratory in Pasadena, California; the Lyndon B. Johnson Space Center in Houston, Texas; and the Langley Research Center in Hampton, Virginia. Headquarters of NASA are in Washington, D.C.

Apollo 11, manned by Buzz Aldrin, Neil A. Armstrong, and Michael Collins, was launched to the Moon on July 16, 1969. Four days later Armstrong and Aldrin landed near the edge of Mare Tranquillitatis. After spending about two hours in gathering rock samples, taking photographs, and setting up scientific equipment for tests, they concluded their lunar surface excursion.

The Apollo Missions

The Apollo program was announced in May 1961, but the choice among competing techniques for achieving a Moon landing and return was not resolved until considerable further study. In the method ultimately employed, a powerful launch vehicle (Saturn V rocket) placed a 50-ton spacecraft in a lunar trajectory. The Apollo spacecraft were supplied with rocket power of their own, which allowed them to brake on approach to the Moon and go into a lunar orbit. They also were able to release a component of the spacecraft, the Lunar Module (LM), carrying its own rocket power, to land two astronauts on the Moon and bring them back to the lunar orbiting Apollo craft.

The first manned Apollo flight was delayed by a tragic accident, a fire that broke out in the Apollo 1 spacecraft during a ground rehearsal on January 27, 1967, killing all three astronauts. On October 11, 1968, following several unmanned Earth-orbit flights, Apollo 7 made a 163-orbit flight carrying a full crew of three astronauts. Apollo 8 carried out the first step of manned lunar exploration; from Earth orbit it was injected into a lunar trajectory, completed lunar orbit, and returned safely to Earth. Apollo 9 carried out a prolonged mission in Earth orbit to check out the LM. Apollo 10 journeyed to lunar orbit and tested the LM to within 15.2 km (50,000 feet) of the Moon's surface. Apollo 11 was the first mission to land on the moon. Apollo 13, launched in April 1970, suffered an accident caused by an explosion in an oxygen tank but returned safely to Earth.

The Apollo 13 Review Board concluded that "all indications are that an electrically initiated fire in oxygen tank No. 2 in the service module (SM) was the cause of the accident." The members felt that "the accident was not the result of a chance malfunction in a statistical sense, but rather resulted from an unusual combination of mistakes, coupled with a somewhat deficient and unforgiving design."

The Cuban Missile Crisis

OXIDIZER TRAILERS

2 MISSILE TRANSPORTERS

OXIDIZER TRAILER

6 MISSILE TRANSPORTERS

PROB IRBM PROPELLANT TRAILERS

ERECTOR

3 MISSILE TRANSPORTERS

Having promised in May 1960 to defend Cuba with Soviet arms, the Soviet premier Nikita Khrushchev assumed that the United States would take no steps to prevent the installation of Soviet medium- and intermediate-range ballistic missiles in Cuba. Such missiles could hit much of the eastern United States within a few minutes if launched from Cuba. The United States learned in July 1962 that the Soviet Union had begun missile shipments to Cuba, and the crisis began.

By August 29, 1962, new military construction and the presence of Soviet technicians had been reported by U.S. U-2 spy planes flying over the island, and on October 14 the presence of a ballistic missile on a launching site was reported.

America Blockades Cuba

After carefully considering the alternatives of an immediate U.S. invasion of Cuba (or air strikes of the missile sites), a blockade of the island, or further diplomatic maneuvers, President John F. Kennedy decided to place a naval "quarantine," or blockade, on Cuba to prevent further Soviet shipments of missiles. Kennedy announced the quarantine on October 22, 1962, and warned that U.S. forces would seize "offensive weapons and associated matériel" that Soviet vessels might attempt to deliver to Cuba. During the following days, Soviet ships bound for Cuba altered course away from the quarantined zone. As the two superpowers hovered close to the brink of nuclear war, messages were exchanged between Kennedy and Khrushchev amidst extreme tension on both sides. On October 28 Khrushchev capitulated, informing Kennedy that work on the missile sites would be halted and that the missiles already in Cuba would be returned to the Soviet Union. In return, Kennedy committed the United States never to invade Cuba. Kennedy also secretly promised to withdraw the nuclear-armed missiles that the United States had stationed in Turkey in previous years. In the following weeks both superpowers began fulfilling their promises, and the crisis was over by late November.

Cuba's communist leader, Fidel Castro, was infuriated by the Soviets' retreat in the face of the U.S. ultimatum but was powerless to act.

The Cuban missile crisis marked the climax of an acutely antagonistic period in U.S.-Soviet relations. The crisis also marked the closest point that the world had ever come to global nuclear war.

John F. Kennedy

Ten months after the Cuban Missile Crisis, Kennedy scored his greatest foreign triumph when Khrushchev and Prime Minister Harold Macmillan of Great Britain joined him in signing the Nuclear Test-Ban Treaty. Yet Kennedy's commitment to combat the spread of communism led him to escalate American involvement in the conflict in Vietnam, where he sent not just supplies and financial assistance, as President Eisenhower had, but 15,000 military advisers as well.

THE VIETNAM WAR

At the heart of the Vietnam War—a protracted conflict that pitted the communist government of North Vietnam and its allies in South Vietnam (the Viet Cong) against the South Vietnam government and its principal ally, the United States—was the desire of North Vietnam, which had defeated the French colonial administration of Vietnam in 1954, to unify the entire country under a single communist regime modeled after those of the Soviet Union and China. The South Vietnamese government, on the other hand, fought to preserve a Vietnam more closely aligned with the West. U.S. military advisers, present in small numbers throughout the 1950s, were introduced on a large scale beginning in 1961, and active combat units were introduced in 1965. By 1969 more than 500,000 U.S. military personnel were stationed in Vietnam. Meanwhile, the Soviet Union and China poured weapons, supplies, and advisers into the North, which in turn provided support, political direction, and regular combat troops for the campaign in the South. The costs and casualties of the growing war proved too much for the United States to bear, and U.S. combat units were withdrawn by 1973. In 1975 Ngo Dinh Diem's South Vietnam fell to a full-scale invasion by the North. The human costs of the long conflict were harsh for all involved. Not until 1995 did Vietnam release its official estimate of war dead: as many as 2 million civilians on both sides and some 1.1 million North Vietnamese and Viet Cong fighters. The U.S. military has estimated that between 200,000 and 250,000 South Vietnamese soldiers died in the war. Nearly 58,200 American soldiers are estimated to have died in the conflict.

The communist National Liberation Front's regular army in South Vietnam was much smaller than Diem's army, but it was only one component of the Viet Cong's so-called People's Liberation Armed Forces (PLAF). At the base of the PLAF were village guerrilla units, made up of part-time combatants who lived at home and worked at their regular occupations during the day.

Vietnam emerged from the war as a potent military power within Southeast Asia, but its agriculture, business, and industry were disrupted, large parts of its countryside were scarred by bombs and defoliation and laced with land mines, and its cities and towns were heavily damaged. A mass exodus in 1975 of people loyal to the South Vietnamese cause was followed by another wave in 1978 of "boat people," refugees fleeing the economic restructuring imposed by the communist regime. Meanwhile, the United States, its military demoralized and its civilian electorate deeply divided, began a process of coming to terms with defeat in what had been its longest and most controversial war.

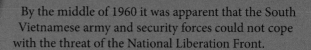

By the middle of 1960 it was apparent that the South Vietnamese army and security forces could not cope with the threat of the National Liberation Front.

The Domino Effect

To the new administration of U.S. Pres. John F. Kennedy, who took office in 1961, Vietnam represented both a challenge and an opportunity. The Viet Cong's armed struggle against Diem seemed to be a prime example of the new Chinese and Soviet strategy of encouraging and aiding "wars of national liberation" in newly independent nations of Asia and Africa—in other words, helping communist-led insurgencies to subvert and overthrow the shaky new governments of emerging nations. Kennedy and some of his close advisers believed that Vietnam presented an opportunity to test the United States' ability to conduct a "counterinsurgency" against communist subversion and guerrilla warfare. Kennedy accepted without serious question the so-called domino theory, which held that the fates of all Southeast Asian countries were closely linked and that a communist success in one must necessarily lead to the fatal weakening of the others.

Effect in America

Disillusionment with the war grew in the U.S. during the 1960s. By 1971, one poll claimed that 71 percent of Americans believed that the United States had "made a mistake" in sending troops to Vietnam and that 58 percent found the war "immoral." Discontent was particularly directed toward the Selective Service System, which had long been seen as unfairly conscripting young men from racial minorities and poor backgrounds while allowing more-privileged men to defer conscription by enrolling in higher education. Nixon ended all draft calls in 1972, and in 1973 the draft was abolished in favor of an all-volunteer military.

The Fall of South Vietnam

In early March of 1975 the North Vietnamese Army (NVA) launched the first phase of what was expected to be a two-year offensive to secure South Vietnam. As it happened, the South's government and army collapsed in less than two months. Gerald R. Ford, who had succeeded Pres. Richard Nixon as U.S. president, pleaded in vain with Congress for additional military aid that might at least raise Saigon's morale. On April 30 what remained of the South Vietnamese government surrendered unconditionally, and NVA tank columns occupied Saigon without a struggle. The remaining Americans escaped in a series of frantic air- and sealifts with Vietnamese friends and coworkers.

A military government was instituted throughout Vietnam, and on July 2, 1976, the country was officially united as the Socialist Republic of Vietnam with its capital in Hanoi.

Social Change & the New Left

The 1960s were marked by the greatest changes in morals and manners in the U.S. since the 1920s. Young people, college students in particular, rebelled against what they viewed as the repressed conformist society of their parents. They advocated a sexual revolution, aided by the birth control pill and later by *Roe* v. *Wade* (1973), a Supreme Court ruling that legalized abortion. "Recreational" drugs such as marijuana and LSD were increasingly used. Opposition to U.S. involvement in Vietnam promoted the rise of a New Left, which was anticapitalist as well as antiwar. The political activists of the New Left drew on the theories of political philosopher Herbert Marcuse, sociologist C. Wright Mills, and psychoanalyst and social philosopher Erich Fromm, among others. A "counterculture" sprang up that legitimized radical standards of taste and behavior in the arts as well as in life. Also, feminism was reborn and joined the ranks of radical causes.

Except for feminism, most organized expressions of the counterculture and the New Left, including the influential Students for a Democratic Society (SDS), did not long survive the 1960s. Nevertheless, they changed American life. Recreational drug taking, previously confined largely to impoverished inner cities, became part of middle-class life. The sexual revolution reduced government censorship, changed attitudes toward traditional sexual roles, and enabled homosexuals to organize and acknowledge their identities as never before. Although there had been earlier protests by gay groups, the Stonewall riots—a series of violent confrontations between police and gay rights activists outside the Stonewall Inn, a bar in New York City, in the summer of 1969—was perhaps the first time lesbians, gays, and transvestites saw the value in uniting behind a common cause. Unrestrained individualism played havoc with family values. People began marrying later and having fewer children. The divorce rate accelerated to the point that the number of divorces per year was roughly half the number of marriages. The number of abortions rose, as did the illegitimacy rate. By the 1980s one in six families was headed by a single woman, and over half of all people living in poverty, including some 12 million children, belonged to such families. Because inflation and recession made it hard to support even intact families on a single income, a majority of mothers entered the workforce. Thus, the stable family-oriented society of the 1950s became a thing of the past.

The New Left

In the United States the New Left grew out of student socialist activism, especially as it intersected with, and was inspired by, the African American civil rights movement.

In theoretical terms, the New Left's major contribution was to a process of revision and diversification within Marxism and related doctrines, especially with regard to concepts of class, agency, ideology, and culture.

The main U.S. New Left organization, Students for a Democratic Society (SDS), was founded in 1959 and issued its political manifesto, *The Port Huron Statement*, in 1962. As American involvement in the Vietnam War escalated, opposition to the war, which was seen as the overarching symbol of Cold War imperialism, became the major focus of American activists and their counterparts elsewhere. New Left movements generally avoided traditional forms of political organization in favor of strategies of mass protest, direct action, and civil disobedience. The high point of New Left activism was reached in 1968 as a wave of radical protest swept across the globe. The revolutionary mood dissipated through the 1970s, although important lines of continuity remained between the New Left and new social movements such as feminism and environmentalism. A minority of activists went on to found clandestine "revolutionary" organizations practicing violent direct action; examples include the Red Army Faction (also known as the Baader-Meinhof Gang) in West Germany and the Weather Underground in the United States. Others moved into far-left parties and groups that proliferated in the 1970s.

The Hippie Movement

Hippies—a countercultural group that originally organized on college campuses—felt alienated from middle-class society, which they saw as dominated by materialism and repression, and they developed their own distinctive lifestyle. Hippies advocated nonviolence and love, a popular phrase being "Make love, not war," for which they were sometimes called "flower children."

The women's movement of the 1960s and 1970s, the so-called "second wave" of feminism, represented a seemingly abrupt break with the tranquil suburban life pictured in American popular culture. Yet the roots of the new rebellion were buried in the frustrations of college-educated mothers whose discontent impelled their daughters in a new direction.

They promoted openness and tolerance as alternatives to the restrictions and regimentation they saw in middle-class society. Hippies often practiced open sexual relationships and lived in various types of family groups. They commonly sought spiritual guidance from sources outside the Judeo-Christian tradition, particularly Buddhism and other Eastern religions, and sometimes in various combinations. Astrology was popular, and the period was often referred to as the Age of Aquarius. Hippies promoted the recreational use of hallucinogenic drugs, particularly marijuana and LSD (lysergic acid diethylamide), in so-called head trips, justifying the practice as a way of expanding consciousness.

Hippies participated in a number of teach-ins at colleges and universities in which opposition to the Vietnam War was explained, and they took part in antiwar protests and marches. They joined other protesters in the "moratorium"—a nationwide demonstration—against the war in 1969.

The Great Society

In Lyndon B. Johnson's first State of the Union message after election in his own right, delivered on January 4, 1965, the president proclaimed his vision of a "Great Society" and pledged to redouble the "war on poverty" he had declared one year earlier. He called for an enormous program of social-welfare legislation, including federal support for education, hospital care for the aged through an expanded Social Security program, and continued enforcement of the Civil Rights Act (1964) and "elimination of the barriers to the right to vote." A majority of the new Congress, elected with Johnson in a Democratic landslide in November 1964, shared the president's vision, and almost all of the Great Society legislation was passed.

The Great Society program, beginning with the Civil Rights Act and continuing with other important measures passed during Johnson's second term, was the most impressive body of social legislation since the New Deal of the 1930s.

The War on Poverty

Johnson also announced an "unconditional war on poverty" in his first State of the Union address. He considered the depth and extent of poverty in the country (nearly 20 percent of Americans at the time were poor) to be a national disgrace that merited a national response. Furthermore, he identified the cause of poverty not as the personal moral failings of the poor but as a societal failure: "The cause may lie deeper in our failure to give our fellow citizens a fair chance to develop their own capacities, in a lack of education and training, in a lack of medical care and housing, in a lack of decent communities in which to live and bring up their children." The speech was historic in its idealistic call for the creation of a more-just society.

The rhetoric of the War on Poverty quickly found its way into law and the creation of new federal programs and agencies. The Economic Opportunity Act of 1964 was passed by Congress and became law in August 1964. The act created the Office of Economic Opportunity (OEO), which provided funds for vocational training, created Job Corps to train youths in conservation camps and urban centers, and established VISTA (Volunteers in Service to America), a domestic counterpart to the Peace Corps, and Head Start, an

Although many of the central programs of the War on Poverty continued well after the 1960s, its legacy remains controversial. Some economists maintain that Johnson's efforts did not achieve a substantial reduction in the rate of poverty; other critics have gone so far as to claim that his programs locked poor people into lives of government dependency, but other scholars dispute those criticisms.

Through year-round residential classroom and work-based learning, Job Corps participants earn a high school diploma or General Educational Development (GED) credential and receive career training in one of many fields, such as business, health, construction, technology, mechanics, and culinary arts.

early-education program for children of poor families, among other programs.

From the outset, Johnson encountered resistance to the War on Poverty from almost all quarters: from the South on issues of race, from conservatives who thought that federal money should not be used to help the poor, and from liberals who thought that the reforms did not go far enough. The War on Poverty was ultimately limited in its effectiveness by the economic resources consumed by the country's increasing involvement in the Vietnam War. As opposition to the war mounted and American society became more polarized over issues of national policy, Johnson's administration was greatly weakened, and he declined to seek reelection in 1968.

In the end, the War on Poverty marked a turning point in American political discourse, and it was later recognized as the high-water mark of American liberalism.

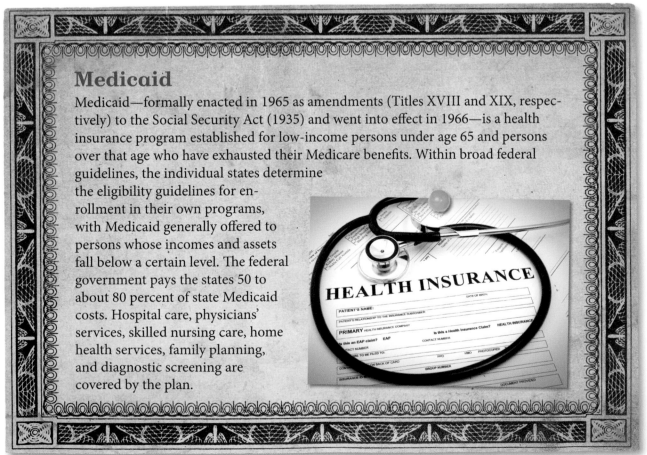

Medicaid

Medicaid—formally enacted in 1965 as amendments (Titles XVIII and XIX, respectively) to the Social Security Act (1935) and went into effect in 1966—is a health insurance program established for low-income persons under age 65 and persons over that age who have exhausted their Medicare benefits. Within broad federal guidelines, the individual states determine the eligibility guidelines for enrollment in their own programs, with Medicaid generally offered to persons whose incomes and assets fall below a certain level. The federal government pays the states 50 to about 80 percent of state Medicaid costs. Hospital care, physicians' services, skilled nursing care, home health services, family planning, and diagnostic screening are covered by the plan.

The Civil Rights Movement

The rising tide of civil rights agitation greatly influenced national opinion and resulted in the passage of the Civil Rights Act of 1964, guaranteeing equal voting rights, outlawing discrimination in restaurants, theaters, and other public accommodations involved in interstate commerce, and encouraging school desegregation.

The Freedom Rides of 1961 signaled the beginning of a period when civil rights protest activity grew in scale and intensity. CORE (Congress of Racial Equality) sponsored the first group of bus riders who sought to desegregate Southern bus terminals. After attacks by white mobs in Alabama turned back the initial protesters, student activists from Nashville and other centers of sit-in activities continued the rides into Jackson, Mississippi, where they were promptly arrested for disobeying racial segregation rules. Despite U.S. Attorney General Robert F. Kennedy's plea for a "cooling-off" period, the Freedom Rides demonstrated that militant but nonviolent young activists could confront Southern segregation at its strongest points and pressure the federal government to intervene to protect the constitutional rights of African Americans. The Freedom Rides encouraged similar protests elsewhere against segregated transportation facilities and stimulated local campaigns in many Southern communities that had been untouched by the student sit-ins.

Similar mass protests in dozens of other cities made white

Americans more aware of the antiquated Jim Crow system, though black militancy also prompted a white "backlash." Those mass protests culminated on August 28, 1963, in the March on Washington for Jobs and Freedom, which attracted over 200,000 participants. Dr. Martin Luther King Jr. used his concluding "I Have a Dream" speech at the march as an opportunity to link black civil rights aspirations with traditional American political values.

Questioning American citizenship and identity as goals for African Americans, black power proponents called instead for a global struggle for black national "self-determination" rather than merely for civil rights.

Militancy and Nonviolence

The passage of voting rights legislation in 1965, the upsurge in Northern urban racial violence, and white resentment of black militancy lessened the effectiveness and popularity of nonviolent protests as a means of advancing African American interests. In addition, the growing militancy of black activists inspired by the then recently assassinated black nationalist Malcolm X spawned an increasing determination among African Americans to achieve political power and cultural autonomy by building black-controlled institutions. When Dr. Martin Luther King Jr. accepted the 1964 Nobel Peace Prize, he connected the African American struggle to the anticolonial struggles that had overcome European domination elsewhere in the world. In 1966 King launched a new campaign in Chicago against Northern slum conditions and segregation, but he soon faced a major challenge from "black power" proponents, such as SNCC (Student Nonviolent Coordinating Committee) chairman Stokely Carmichael. This ideological conflict came to a head in June 1966 during a voting rights march through Mississippi following the wounding of James Meredith, who had desegregated the University of Mississippi in 1962. Carmichael's use of the "black power" slogan encapsulated the emerging notion of a freedom struggle seeking political, economic, and cultural objectives beyond narrowly defined civil rights reforms. By the late 1960s not only the NAACP (National Association for the Advancement of Colored People) and SCLC (Southern Christian Leadership Conference) but even SNCC and CORE faced challenges from new militant organizations, such as the Black Panther Party, whose leaders argued that civil rights reforms were insufficient because they did not fully address the problems of poor and powerless blacks. They also dismissed nonviolent principles.

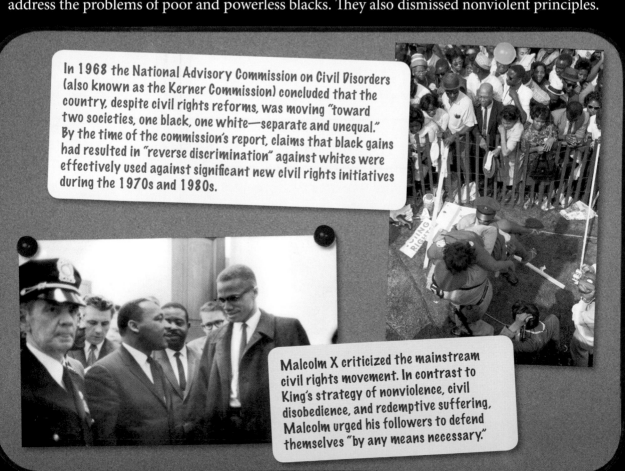

In 1968 the National Advisory Commission on Civil Disorders (also known as the Kerner Commission) concluded that the country, despite civil rights reforms, was moving "toward two societies, one black, one white—separate and unequal." By the time of the commission's report, claims that black gains had resulted in "reverse discrimination" against whites were effectively used against significant new civil rights initiatives during the 1970s and 1980s.

Malcolm X criticized the mainstream civil rights movement. In contrast to King's strategy of nonviolence, civil disobedience, and redemptive suffering, Malcolm urged his followers to defend themselves "by any means necessary."

The Women's Rights MOVEMENT

In the aftermath of World War II, the lives of women in developed countries changed dramatically. Household technology eased the burdens of homemaking, life expectancies increased dramatically, and the growth of the service sector opened up thousands of jobs not dependent on physical strength. Despite these socioeconomic transformations, cultural attitudes (especially concerning women's work) and legal precedents still reinforced sexual inequalities.

The first public indication that change was imminent came with women's reaction to the 1963 publication of Betty Friedan's *The Feminine Mystique*. Friedan spoke of the problem that "lay buried, unspoken" in the minds of the suburban housewife: utter boredom and lack of fulfillment. Women who had been told that they had it all—nice houses, lovely children, responsible husbands—were deadened by domesticity, she said, and they were too socially conditioned to recognize their own desperation. *The Feminine Mystique* was an immediate best seller. Friedan had struck a chord.

Friedan argued that when men returned home after the war, women—who had stepped in to fill the jobs men had left in order to fight in the war—were expected to return to the home and to perform more-suitable "feminine" activities.

Initially, women energized by Friedan's book joined with government leaders and union

representatives who had been lobbying the federal government for equal pay and for protection against employment discrimination. By June 1966, they had concluded that polite requests were insufficient. They would need their own national pressure group—a women's equivalent of the National Association for the Advancement of Colored People. With this, the National Organization for Women (NOW) was born.

Successes and Failures

Despite dissension in its leadership and ranks, the women's movement achieved much in a short period of time. With the eventual backing of the Equal Employment Opportunity

A broad social movement for the relaxation or elimination of restrictions on the performance of abortions resulted in the passing of liberalized legislation in several states in the United States during the 1960s.

Commission (1965), women gained access to jobs in every corner of the U.S. economy, and employers with long histories of discrimination were required to provide timetables for increasing the number of women in their workforces. Divorce laws were liberalized; employers were barred from firing pregnant women; and women's studies programs were created in colleges and universities. Record numbers of women ran for—and started winning—political office. In 1972, Congress passed Title IX of the Higher Education Act, which prohibited discrimination on the basis of sex in any educational program receiving federal funds and thereby forced all-male schools to open their doors to women and athletic programs to sponsor and finance female sports teams. And in 1973, in its controversial ruling on *Roe* v. *Wade*, the United States Supreme Court legalized abortion.

The National Organization for Women was established by a small group of feminists who were dedicated to actively challenging sex discrimination in all areas of American society but particularly in employment.

Political movements, however, rarely last more than a decade, and the dwindling of the women's movement was hastened by NOW's singular focus on the passage of the Equal Rights Amendment. Led by women such as Bella Abzug, Betty Friedan, and Gloria Steinem, the ERA passed Congress in 1972. But its ratification by the states became a rallying point for the backlash against feminism. Needing 38 states to ratify within 10 years of its passage by Congress, the amendment fell three states short.

The failure of the ERA was followed by the gradual demise of organized, often bellicose activity by masses of women in the United States. Moreover, there was a growing national sense that the core goals of the women's movement had been achieved. NOW continued to work for women's rights into the new millennium—to defend abortion rights (a cause made more prominent by the National Abortion Rights Action League) and sexual harassment laws, to promote full equality in the military (including combat duty), and to secure greater federal funding for child care and for programs to prevent violence against women. But despite NOW's growth, both in budget and in membership, its activism became fragmented and fraught with dissension.

While the first-wave feminism of the 19th and early 20th centuries focused on women's legal rights, such as the right to vote, the second-wave feminism of the "women's movement" peaked in the 1960s and 1970s and touched on every area of women's experience —including family, sexuality, and work.

THE WAR ON DRUGS

The War on Drugs was a relatively small component of federal law-enforcement efforts until the presidency of Ronald Reagan, which began in 1981. Reagan greatly expanded the reach of the drug war and his focus on criminal punishment over treatment led to a massive increase in incarcerations for nonviolent drug offenses, from 50,000 in 1980 to 400,000 in 1997. In 1984 his wife, Nancy, spearheaded another facet of the War on Drugs with her "Just Say No" campaign, which was a privately funded effort to educate schoolchildren on the dangers of drug use. The expansion of the War on Drugs was in many ways driven by increased media coverage of—and resulting public nervousness over—the crack epidemic that arose in the early 1980s. This heightened concern over illicit drug use helped drive political support for Reagan's hard-line stance on drugs. The U.S. Congress passed the Anti-Drug Abuse Act of 1986, which allocated $1.7 billion to the War on Drugs and established a series of "mandatory minimum" prison sentences for various drug offenses. A notable feature of mandatory minimums was the massive gap between the amounts of crack and of powder cocaine that resulted in the same minimum sentence: possession of five grams of crack led to an automatic five-year sentence while it took the possession of 500 grams of powder cocaine to trigger that sentence. Since approximately 80 percent of crack users were African American, mandatory minimums led to an unequal increase of incarceration rates for nonviolent black drug offenders, as well as claims that the War on Drugs was a racist institution.

Emergency room visits due to cocaine incidents such as overdoses, unexpected reactions, suicide attempts, chronic effects, and detoxification increased fourfold between 1984 and 1987.

Concerns over the effectiveness of the War on Drugs and increased awareness of the racial disparity of the punishments meted out by it led to decreased public support of the most draconian aspects of the drug war during the early 21st century. Consequently, reforms were enacted during that time, such as the legalization of recreational marijuana in a number of states and the passage of the Fair Sentencing Act of 2010 that reduced the discrepancy of crack-to-powder possession thresholds for minimum sentences from 100-to-1 to 18-to-1. While the War on Drugs is still technically being waged, it is done at much less intense levels than it was during its peak in the 1980s.

Nancy Reagan was often credited with influencing personnel decisions (both hiring and firing), setting her husband's travel schedule, and shaping his agenda. Her leadership in the "Just Say No" campaign increased her popularity.

The War on Drugs resulted in an immense growth in court caseloads and the prison population. The War on Drugs focused on small-time drug dealers, who were generally poor young black males from the inner city.

The Crack Epidemic

Cocaine hydrochloride—powdered cocaine—was a major cash crop for South American countries, especially Colombia. Until the 1960s, very few people knew about cocaine, and the demand was limited. As the desire for the drug increased, Colombian trafficking organizations such as the Medellín cartel instituted a distribution system that imported cocaine from South America into the U.S. market using sea and air routes via the Caribbean and the South Florida coast. Trafficking organizations oversaw all operations, including the conversion, packaging, transportation, and first-level distribution of cocaine in the United States.

Crack cocaine first appeared in Miami, where Caribbean immigrants taught adolescents the technique of converting powdered cocaine into crack. The teenagers eventually introduced the business of producing and distributing crack cocaine into other major cities of the United States, including New York City, Detroit, and Los Angeles.

The initiation of crack cocaine into socially eroded communities took place during President Ronald Reagan's term in office, when there was a structural shift that caused huge manufacturing industries to move outside the cities. Their relocation created workforce competitions that further widened the gap between social and economic segments in the inner cities of America. But few skills and resources were needed to sell crack. Many small-time drug dealers worked independently and outside the control of organizations like the Medellín cartel. The rewards clearly outweighed the risks. A small-time drug dealer who sold crack daily earned a median net income of $2,000 per month. The increase in the demand for crack cocaine caused intense competition between drug dealers as they fought to profit from the same customers. Consequently, violence became linked to crack cocaine as these small-time drug dealers defended their economic boundaries.

The emergence of crack cocaine in the inner cities led to a drastic increase in crime between 1981 and 1986. Federal prison admission for drug offenses soared, and murder and nonnegligent manslaughter rates increased significantly. There were also marked increases in robbery and aggravated assault.

Ultimately, the prison population doubled due to the arrest of drug dealers and their customers. One in every four African American males aged 20 to 29 was either incarcerated or on probation or parole by 1989, which contributed to the United States' having the highest incarceration rate in the world. By 1995, that statistic had increased to nearly one in three.

THE PERSIAN GULF WAR

The allied coalition's military offensive against Iraq began on January 16–17, 1991, with a massive U.S.-led air campaign that continued through-out the war.

On August 2, 1990, Iraq's leader, Saddam Hussein, ordered the invasion and occupation of Kuwait with the apparent aim of acquiring that nation's large oil reserves, canceling a large debt Iraq owed Kuwait, and expanding Iraqi power in the region. On August 3 the United Nations Security Council called for Iraq to withdraw from Kuwait, and on August 6 the council imposed a worldwide ban on trade with Iraq. (The Iraqi government responded by formally annexing Kuwait on August 8.) Iraq's invasion and the potential threat it then posed to Saudi Arabia, the world's largest oil producer and exporter, prompted the United States and its western European NATO allies to rush troops to Saudi Arabia to deter a possible attack. Egypt and several other Arab nations joined the anti-Iraq coalition and contributed forces to the military buildup, known as Operation Desert Shield. Iraq meanwhile built up its occupying army in Kuwait to about 300,000 troops.

On November 29 the UN Security Council authorized the use of force against Iraq if it did not withdraw from Kuwait by January 15, 1991. By January 1991 the allied coalition against Iraq had reached a strength of 700,000 troops, including 540,000 U.S. personnel and smaller numbers of British, French, Egyptians, Saudis, Syrians, and several other national contingents. Saddam steadfastly refused to withdraw Iraqi forces from Kuwait, however, which he maintained would remain a province of Iraq.

The sustained aerial bombardment, which had been named Operation Desert Storm, destroyed Iraq's air defenses before attacking its communications networks, government buildings, weapons plants, oil refineries, and bridges and roads. By mid-February the allies had shifted their air attacks to Iraq's forward ground forces in Kuwait and southern Iraq, destroying their fortifications and tanks.

Operation Desert Sabre

Operation Desert Sabre, a massive allied ground offensive, was launched northward from northeastern Saudi Arabia into Kuwait and southern Iraq on February 24, and within three days Arab and U.S. forces had retaken Kuwait city in the face of crumbling Iraqi resistance. Meanwhile, the main U.S. armored thrust drove into Iraq some 120 miles (200 km) west of Kuwait and attacked Iraq's armored reserves from the rear. By February 27 these forces had destroyed most of Iraq's elite Republican Guard units after the latter had tried to make a stand south of Al-Baṣrah in southeastern Iraq. By the time that U.S. President George Bush declared a cease-fire for February 28, Iraqi resistance had completely collapsed.

There are no official figures for the Iraqi military operation. Estimates of the number of Iraqi troops in the Kuwait theater range from 180,000 to 630,000, and estimates of Iraqi military deaths range from 8,000 to 100,000. The allies, by contrast, lost about 300 troops in the conflict.

Peace Agreement and Aftermath

The terms of the peace were, *inter alia*, that Iraq recognize Kuwait's sovereignty and that it divest itself of all weapons of mass destruction (i.e., nuclear, biological, and chemical weapons) and all missiles with ranges exceeding 90 miles (150 km). Pending complete compliance, economic sanctions would continue.

In the aftermath of Iraq's defeat, Kurds in the north of the country and Shīʿites in the south rose in a rebellion that was suppressed by Saddam with great brutality. These actions prompted the allies to prohibit Iraqi aircraft from operating in designated "no-fly" zones over these areas. As the other allies gradually left the coalition, U.S. and British aircraft continued to patrol Iraqi skies, and UN inspectors sought to guarantee that all illicit weapons were destroyed. Iraq's failure to cooperate with inspectors led in 1998 to a brief resumption of hostilities (Operation Desert Fox). Iraq thereafter refused to readmit inspectors into the country, and regular exchanges of fire between Iraqi forces and U.S. and British aircraft over the no-fly zones continued into the 21st century.

Iraq's crushing defeat triggered internal rebellions by both Shīʿites and Kurds, but Saddam suppressed their uprisings, causing thousands to flee to refugee camps along the country's northern border. Untold thousands more were murdered, many simply disappearing into the regime's prisons.

North American
FREE TRADE AGREEMENT

The North American Free Trade Agreement (NAFTA) was inspired by the success of the European Economic Community (1957–93) in eliminating tariffs in order to stimulate trade among its members. Proponents argued that establishing a free-trade area in North America would bring prosperity through increased trade and production, resulting in the creation of millions of well-paying jobs in all participating countries.

A Canadian-U.S. free-trade agreement was concluded in 1988, and NAFTA basically extended that agreement's provisions to Mexico. NAFTA was negotiated by the administrations of U.S. Pres. George H.W. Bush, Canadian Prime Minister Brian Mulroney, and Mexican Pres. Carlos Salinas de Gortari. A preliminary agreement on the pact was reached in August 1992, and it was signed by the three leaders on December 17. NAFTA was ratified by the three countries' national legislatures in 1993 and went into effect on January 1, 1994.

NAFTA's main provisions called for the gradual reduction of tariffs, customs duties, and other trade barriers between the three members, with some tariffs being removed immediately and others over periods of as long as 15 years.

Provisions

NAFTA ensured eventual duty-free access for a vast range of manufactured goods and commodities traded between the signatories. "National goods" status was provided to products imported from other NAFTA countries, banning any state, local, or provincial government from imposing taxes or tariffs on such goods.

NAFTA also contained provisions aimed at securing intellectual-property rights. Participating countries would adhere to rules protecting intellectual property and would adopt strict measures against industrial theft. Other provisions instituted formal rules for resolving disputes between investors and participating countries. Among other things,

Environmentalists were concerned about the potentially disastrous effects of rapid industrialization in Mexico, given that country's lack of experience in implementing and enforcing environmental regulations. Potential environmental problems were addressed in the North American Agreement on Environmental Cooperation in 1994.

such rules permitted corporations or individual investors to sue for compensation any signatory country that violated the rules of the treaty.

Additional side agreements were adopted to address concerns over the potential labor-market and environmental impacts of the treaty. Critics worried that generally low wages in Mexico would attract U.S. and Canadian companies, resulting in a production shift to Mexico and a rapid decline in manufacturing jobs in the United States and Canada.

Criticism and Effects

Many critics of NAFTA viewed the agreement as a radical experiment engineered by influential multinational corporations seeking to increase their profits at the expense of the ordinary citizens of the countries involved. Opposition groups argued that overarching rules imposed by NAFTA could undermine local governments by preventing them from issuing laws or regulations designed to protect the public interest. Critics also argued that the treaty would bring about a major degradation in environmental and health standards, promote the privatization and deregulation of key public services, and displace family farmers in signatory countries.

NAFTA produced mixed results. It turned out to be neither the magic bullet that its proponents had envisioned nor the devastating blow that its critics had predicted. Mexico did experience a dramatic increase in its exports, from about $60 billion in 1994 to nearly $400 billion by 2013. The surge in exports was accompanied by an explosion in imports as well, resulting in an influx of better-quality and lower-priced goods for Mexican consumers.

Economic growth during the post-NAFTA period was not impressive in any of the countries involved. The United States and Canada suffered greatly from several economic recessions, including the Great Recession of 2007–09, overshadowing any beneficial effects that NAFTA could have brought about. Mexico's gross domestic product (GDP) grew at a lower rate compared with that of other Latin American countries such as Brazil and Chile, and its growth in income per person also was not significant, though there was an expansion of the middle class in the post-NAFTA years.

Little happened in the labor market that dramatically changed the outcomes in any country involved in the treaty. Because of immigration restrictions, the wage gap between Mexico on the one hand and the United States and Canada on the other did not shrink. The lack of infrastructure in Mexico caused many U.S. and Canadian firms to choose not to invest directly in that country. As a result, there were no significant job losses in the U.S. and Canada and no environmental disaster caused by industrialization in Mexico.

According to many experts, the Trans-Pacific Partnership (TPP) that was signed on October 5, 2015, constituted an expansion of NAFTA on a much larger scale.

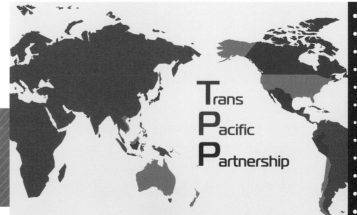

Trans Pacific Partnership

- Australia
- Brunei
- Canada
- Chile
- Malaysia
- Mexico
- New Zealand
- Peru
- Singapore
- United States
- Vietnam
- Japan

The Attacks of
SEPTEMBER 11, 2001

On September 11, 2001, groups of attackers boarded four domestic aircraft at three East Coast airports, and soon after takeoff they disabled the crews, some of whom may have been stabbed with box cutters the hijackers were secreting. The hijackers then took control of the aircraft, all large and bound for the West Coast with full loads of fuel. At 8:46 am the first plane, American Airlines flight 11, which had originated from Boston, was piloted into the north tower of the World Trade Center in New York City. Most observers construed this initially to be an accident involving a small commuter plane. The second plane, United Airlines flight 175, also from Boston, struck the south tower 17 minutes later. At this point there was no doubt that the United States was under attack. Each structure was badly damaged by the impact and erupted into flames. Office workers who were trapped above the points of impact in some cases leapt to their deaths rather than face the infernos now raging inside the towers. The third plane, American Airlines flight 77, taking off from Dulles Airport near Washington, D.C., struck the southwest side of the Pentagon at 9:37 am, touching off a fire in that section of the structure. Minutes later the Federal Aviation Authority ordered a nationwide ground stop, and within the next hour (at 10:03 am) the fourth aircraft, United Airlines flight 93 from Newark, New Jersey, crashed near Shanksville in the Pennsylvania countryside after its passengers—informed of events via cellular phone—attempted to overpower their assailants.

If al-Qaeda had been a largely unknown organization before September 11, in the days after it became a household name.

At 9:59 am the World Trade Center's heavily damaged south tower collapsed, and the north tower fell 29 minutes later. Clouds of smoke and debris quickly filled the streets of Lower Manhattan. Office workers and residents ran in panic as they tried to outpace the billowing debris clouds. A number of other buildings adjacent to the twin towers suffered serious damage, and several subsequently fell. Fires at the World Trade Center site smoldered for more than three months.

The September 11 attacks were an enormous tactical success for al-Qaeda—a broad-based militant Islamist organization founded by Osama bin Laden in the late 1980s. The strikes were well coordinated and hit multiple targets in the heart of the enemy, and the attacks were magnified by being broadcast around the world to an audience of untold millions. The September 11 "propaganda of the deed" took place in the media capital of the world, which ensured the widest possible coverage of the event.

The War on Terrorism

The War on Terrorism was launched in response to the terrorist attacks of September 11, 2001. It is a multidimensional campaign of almost limitless scope. Its military dimension has involved major wars in Afghanistan and Iraq, covert operations in Yemen and elsewhere, large-scale military-assistance programs for cooperative regimes, and major increases in military spending. Its intelligence dimension has comprised institutional reorganization and considerable increases in the funding of America's intelligence-gathering capabilities, a global program of capturing terrorist suspects and interning them at Guantánamo Bay, expanded cooperation with foreign intelligence agencies, and the tracking and interception of terrorist financing. Its diplomatic dimension includes continuing efforts to construct and maintain a global coalition of partner states and organizations and an extensive public diplomacy campaign to counter anti-Americanism in the Middle East. The domestic dimension of the U.S. war on terrorism has entailed new anti-terrorism legislation, such as the USA PATRIOT Act; new security institutions, such as the Department of Homeland Security; the preventive detainment of thousands of suspects; surveillance and intelligence-gathering programs by the National Security Agency (NSA), the Federal Bureau of Investigation (FBI), and local authorities; the strengthening of emergency-response procedures; and increased security measures for airports, borders, and public events.

Some 2,750 people were killed in New York, 184 at the Pentagon, and 40 in Pennsylvania from the September 11 attacks; all 19 terrorists died as well.

The USA PATRIOT Act

In the wake of the September 11 attacks, the administration of Pres. George W. Bush submitted to Congress draft legislation designed to expand the powers of the government to surveil, investigate, and detain suspected terrorists. Some key provisions of the legislation consisted of amendments to the Wiretap Act (1968; amended 1986 and 1994), which had prohibited eavesdropping by the government on private face-to-face, telephone, and electronic communications except as authorized by court order in narrowly defined circumstances in cases of serious crimes. Sections 201 and 202 of the USA PATRIOT Act added computer and terrorist crimes to the list of serious offenses in connection with which law-enforcement officials could seek a court order to conduct eavesdropping. Section 209 established that voice mail was not entitled to the same protections that governed telephone conversations but only to the weaker safeguards applicable to telephone records and e-mail stored with third parties (usually an Internet service provider). In Section 210 the act added individual subscribers' credit card or bank account numbers to records that could be obtained from a communication services provider through a subpoena.

Police and fire departments in New York were especially hard-hit: hundreds had rushed to the scene of the attacks, and more than 400 police officers and firefighters were killed.

THE AFGHANISTAN WAR

The Afghanistan War was an international conflict in Afghanistan that was triggered by the September 11 attacks. The campaign in Afghanistan started covertly on September 26, 2001, with a CIA team known as Jawbreaker arriving in the country and, working with anti-Taliban allies, initiating a strategy for overthrowing the Taliban regime—an ultraconservative Islamic political and religious faction that ruled Afghanistan. U.S. officials hoped that by partnering with the Afghans they could avoid deploying a large force to Afghanistan. Pentagon officials were especially concerned that the United States not be drawn into a protracted occupation of Afghanistan, as had occurred with the Soviets more than two decades prior. The United States relied primarily on the Northern Alliance, a loose coalition of Islamic guerrilla militias who controlled northern Afghanistan, which had just lost its commander Ahmad Shah Massoud but had regrouped under other commanders, including Tajik leader Mohammed Fahim and Abdul Rashid Dostum, an Uzbek. The Americans also teamed with anti-Taliban Pashtuns in southern Afghanistan, including a little-known tribal leader named Hamid Karzai.

Prior to the killing of al-Qaeda leader Osama bin Laden by U.S. forces in 2011, the Americans were believed to have come closest to bin Laden in the December 2001 battle of Tora Bora (bin Laden's mountain stronghold). But bin Laden was thought to have managed to have slipped into Pakistan with the help of Afghan and Pakistani forces that were supposedly helping the Americans.

The CIA team was soon joined by U.S. and British special forces contingents, and together they provided arms, equipment, and advice to the Afghans. They also helped coordinate targeting for the air campaign, which began on Oct. 7, 2001, with U.S. and British war planes pounding Taliban targets, thus marking the public start of Operation Enduring Freedom. In late October, Northern Alliance forces began to overtake a series of towns formerly held by the Taliban. The forces worked with U.S. assistance, but they defied U.S. wishes when, on November 13, they marched into Kabul as the Taliban retreated without a fight. Kandahar, the largest city in southern Afghanistan and the Taliban's spiritual home, fell on December 6, marking the end of Taliban power in Afghanistan. It had been besieged by a force led by Karzai that moved in from the north and one commanded by Gul Agha Sherzai that advanced from the south; both operated with heavy assistance from the United States. As the Taliban leadership retreated into Afghanistan's rural areas and across the border to Pakistan, anti-Taliban figures convened at a United Nations sponsored conference in Bonn, Germany. With behind-the-scenes maneuvering by the United States, Karzai was selected to lead the country on an interim basis.

The Iraq War

In 2002 the U.S. president, George W. Bush, argued that the vulnerability of the United States following the September 11 attacks of 2001, combined with Iraq's alleged continued possession and manufacture of weapons of mass destruction (an accusation that was later proved erroneous) and its support for terrorist groups—which, according to the Bush administration, included al-Qaeda, the perpetrators of the September 11 attacks—made disarming Iraq a renewed priority.

U.S. and allied forces launched an attack on the morning of March 20; it began when U.S. aircraft dropped several precision-guided bombs on a bunker complex in which the Iraqi president, Saddam Hussein, was believed to be meeting with senior staff. This was followed by a series of air strikes directed against government and military installations, and within days U.S. forces had invaded Iraq from Kuwait in the south. Despite fears that Iraqi forces would engage in a scorched-earth policy—destroying bridges and dams and setting fire to Iraq's southern oil wells—little damage was done by retreating Iraqi forces; in fact, large numbers of Iraqi troops simply chose not to resist the advance of coalition forces. In southern Iraq the greatest resistance to U.S. forces as they advanced northward was from irregular groups of Ba'th Party—the Arab political party under Hussein's rule that advocated the formation of a single Arab socialist nation—supporters, known as Saddam's Fedayeen.

The opening salvo of the Iraq War was an assault by U.S. aircraft on a bunker complex in which Saddam was thought to be meeting with subordinates. Although the attack failed to kill the Iraqi leader, subsequent attacks directed against Saddam made it clear that eliminating him was a major goal of the invasion.

Saddam's hometown of Tikrit, the last major stronghold of the regime, fell with little resistance on April 13, 2003. Isolated groups of regime loyalists continued to fight on subsequent days, but the U.S. president declared an end to major combat on May 1. Iraqi leaders fled into hiding and were the object of an intense search by U.S. forces. Saddam Hussein was captured on December 13, 2003, and was turned over to Iraqi authorities in June 2004 to stand trial for various crimes; he was subsequently convicted of crimes against humanity and was executed on December 30, 2006.

In February 2009 newly elected U.S. Pres. Barack Obama announced that U.S. combat forces would be withdrawn from Iraq by August 31, 2010, with the remaining troops due to pull out by the end of 2011. On August 18, 2010—two weeks ahead of schedule—the last combat brigade withdrew from Iraq; 50,000 U.S. soldiers remained in Iraq to act as a transitional force.

The Great Recession

The devastation to the U.S. economy spread far beyond housing. The banking industry was especially hard hit. Altogether, 176 banks in the U.S. failed in 2009, many of them small and local.

In 2008, the U.S. housing market was the domino that, when it fell, toppled many of the world's major economies and led the world into recession. For the first half of the decade, aggressive investing by homebuyers, mortgage lenders, Wall Street investment houses, and insurers had driven up the median price of a single-family home by almost 10 percent a year, with housing in some parts of the country escalating even faster. When home prices headed back down in 2007, large numbers of homeowners faced rising adjustable-rate mortgage payments and/or could no longer borrow against a rising home value to finance other expenses. By the middle of 2009, the median home price had fallen close to its 2000 level. Those with heavy investments in housing, including risky mortgage-backed securities, found them all but worthless. The government stepped in with a massively expensive bailout program in late 2008 and continuing into 2009.

The Government Takes Action

As 2009 began, comparisons with the Great Depression were as common as foreclosed houses in Nevada, but there was one important difference: policy makers this time had the experience of the Depression to guide them. They identified three policy areas where they vowed not to make the same mistakes that seemed to have prolonged the Depression: fiscal, monetary, and trade.

In the 1930s, national leaders generally pledged allegiance to fiscal policies based on balanced budgets. With tax revenue falling in tandem with economic growth, balancing budgets meant cutting spending just when economies needed to stimulate business expansion and job growth. This time around, however, political leaders poured money into such projects as road construction and schools. Although some governments were more aggressive than others, just about all countries joined the stimulus parade.

In 1929 the U.S. Federal Reserve Board (Fed), seeking to restrain a speculative rise in stock prices, instituted a monetary policy of tight money and high interest rates. The economy predictably contracted, and the Depression officially began that August. Nevertheless, the Fed further tightened its grip on the money supply in 1931, adding to the squeeze on the domestic economy. Through all of 2009, however, the Fed held the Fed Funds rate (the interest rate that banks pay each other for overnight loans) in a range of 0.0–0.25 percent. Most other central banks also loosened monetary policy. The Fed and many of its foreign counterparts also injected capital into banks and bought their shaky loans.

Even financially secure banks, not trusting potential borrowers to pay them back, stopped lending. Businesses—especially small and new businesses—could not find the credit that they needed to pay creditors or buy inventory or to pay their own workers, much less to hire new ones. Even short-term interest rates close to zero did not fully thaw credit markets.

Enlightened decision making may have blocked another Depression, but it could not prevent a great deal of misery. The financial crisis struck individual countries with an impact that depended heavily on two factors: whether local institutions had ties to the U.S. financial sector and whether the local economy depended on export sales to the West.

The Numbers

The Great Recession (which officially dated from December 2007 to June 2009 in the United States), included the most dismal two-quarter period for the U.S. economy in more than 60 years: GDP contracted by 8.9 percent in the fourth quarter of 2008 and by 6.7 percent in the first quarter of 2009. Efforts to stabilize the economy included extending $80 billion to automakers Chrysler and General Motors, with the government assuming ownership of 8 percent and 61 percent of each, respectively; the Federal Reserve pumping well over $1 trillion into the economy by purchasing Treasury bonds; and the passage of a $787 billion stimulus spending measure. In the third quarter of 2009, GDP finally turned positive, gaining 2.2 percent on an annualized basis. However, unemployment, which had stood at 7.2 percent at the beginning of the year, hovered around 10 percent in early 2010. Moreover, the stimulative policies had helped balloon the U.S. federal deficit to $1.42 trillion, earning widespread criticism from Republicans.

U.S. STATES

Alabama	Alabama was admitted in 1819 as the 22nd state. Montgomery is the state capital. Alabama was the birthplace of author Helen Keller, musician Hank Williams, and activist Rosa Parks. Population (2010) 4,779,736; (2016 est.) 4,863,300.	
Alaska	Alaska was admitted to the union as the 49th state on January 3, 1959. The capital is Juneau, which lies in the southeast, in the panhandle region. For at least one day in summer, the Sun never sets on the northern parts of Alaska. Population (2010) 710,231; (2016 est.) 741,894.	
Arizona	Arizona achieved statehood on February 14, 1912, the last of the 48 conterminous United States to be admitted to the union. Phoenix, situated in the south-central part of the state, is the capital and largest city. Arizona has more national parks and monuments than any other state. Population (2010) 6,392,017; (2016 est.) 6,931,071.	
Arkansas	For more than a century after Arkansas was admitted as the 25th member of the United States in 1836. Little Rock, the state capital, is located in the central part of the state. Arkansas ranks 29th among the 50 states in total area, but, except for Louisiana and Hawaii, it is the smallest state west of the Mississippi River. Population (2010) 2,915,918; (2016 est.) 2,988,248.	
California	California, was admitted as the 31st state of the union on September 9, 1850, and by the early 1960s it was the most populous U.S. state. The capital is Sacramento. California is the most biologically diverse state in the United States, with more than 40,000 plant and animal species, some of which are endangered or threatened. Population (2010) 37,253,956; (2015 est.) 39,250,017.	
Colorado	Colorado was admitted to the union on August 1, 1876, as the 38th state. The capital is Denver. Colorado ranks first of all U.S. states in the average height above sea level of its land. Population (2010) 5,029,196; (2016 est.) 5,540,545.	
Connecticut	Connecticut was one of the original 13 states and is one of the six New England states. The capital is Hartford. It ranks 48th among the 50 U.S. states in terms of total area but is among the most densely populated. Population (2010) 3,574,097; (2016 est.) 3,576,452.	
Delaware	Delaware was the first of the original 13 states to ratify the federal Constitution. The capital is Dover. Delaware is the legal home to thousands of American and foreign corporations. More than three-fifths of the companies listed on the New York Stock Exchange are incorporated in Delaware. Population (2010) 897,934; (2016 est.) 952,065.	
Florida	Florida was admitted as the 27th state in 1845. The capital is Tallahassee. Florida has regularly ranked among the states with the fastest-growing immigrant population. Population (2010) 18,801,310; (2016 est.) 20,612,439.	
Georgia	Georgia was one of the original 13 states. Georgia was founded in 1732. The capital is Atlanta. Georgia is one of the country's major producers of building stone and crushed stone, as well as cement, sand, and gravel. Population (2010) 9,687,653; (2016 est.) 10,310,371.	

Hawaii	Hawaii became the 50th U.S. state on August 21, 1959. Hawaii is a group of volcanic islands in the central Pacific Ocean. The capital is Honolulu, located on the island of Oahu. Mount Waialeale, on Kauai, gets more rain—450 inches per year—than almost any other place on Earth. Population (2010) 1,360,301; (2016 est.) 1,428,557.	
Idaho	Idaho, admitted as the 43rd state of the union on July 3, 1890, is one of the Mountain states. Boise is the state capital. The residents of Idaho enjoy some of the largest unspoiled natural areas in the United States, including about 3,900 square miles (10,000 square km) of wilderness and primitive land in which roads and vehicles are seldom to be found. Population (2010) 1,567,582; (2016 est.) 1,683,140.	
Illinois	Admitted as the 21st member of the union on December 3, 1818, Illinois lies within both the so-called old industrial belt and the fertile agricultural heart of the country. The capital is Springfield, in the west-central part of the state. Hundreds of years ago, the largest city north of Mexico was at Cahokia, now in Illinois. Population (2010) 12,830,632; (2016 est.) 12,801,539.	
Indiana	Indiana was admitted on December 11, 1816, as the 19th state of the union. Its capital has been at Indianapolis since 1825. Indiana has contributed to popular literature in the United States through such wordsmiths as poet James Whitcomb Riley and novelists Booth Tarkington, Lew Wallace, and Kurt Vonnegut, Jr. Population (2010) 6,483,802; (2016 est.) 6,633,053.	
Iowa	Iowa was admitted to the union as the 29th state on December 28, 1846. Des Moines, in the south-central part of the state, is the capital. Iowa is one of the leading U.S. states in number of farms. More than nine-tenths of its land is devoted to agriculture, making it one of the top states in agricultural production. Population (2010) 3,046,355; (2016 est.) 3,134,693.	
Kansas	Kansas became the 34th state on January 29, 1861. In that year the capital was located in Topeka by popular election. Kansas has an extensive system of state parks and recreation areas, many of them associated with reservoirs. There are no national parks or monuments in the state. Population (2010) 2,853,118; (2016 est.) 2,907,289.	
Kentucky	By 1792, when Kentucky was admitted as the 15th state of the union—the first west of the Appalachian Mountains—it had drawn nearly 73,000 settlers. The capital is Frankfort. The vast majority of Kentucky's farms are owned by individuals or families (as opposed to corporations), and almost one-fifth of the state's total workforce is employed in farm or farm-related jobs. Population (2010) 4,339,367; (2016 est.) 4,436,974.	
Louisiana	Admitted to the union in 1812 as the 18th state, Louisiana commands a once strategically vital region. Its capital is Baton Rouge. Louisiana is the only U.S. state where the counties are called parishes. Population (2010) 4,533,372; (2016 est.) 4,681,666.	
Maine	Maine was admitted to the union on March 15, 1820, as the 23rd state; its capital is Augusta. Maine is the most sparsely populated state east of the Mississippi River. More than four-fifths of its total land area is under forest cover. Population (2010) 1,328,361; (2016 est.) 1,331,479.	
Maryland	Maryland was one of the original 13 states. It lies at the center of the Eastern Seaboard. Annapolis, the state capital, lies on Chesapeake Bay. The state's crab haul consistently has surpassed that of other states, although there has been a marked decline in the catch since the late 1990s. Population (2010) 5,773,552; (2016 est.) 6,016,447.	

Massachusetts	Massachusetts was one of the original 13 states and is one of the six New England states. The capital is Boston. In 2004 Massachusetts became the first state to legalize same-sex marriage. Population (2010) 6,547,629; (2016 est.) 6,811,779.	
Michigan	Michigan was admitted as a state on January 26, 1837, as the 26th state of the union and the fourth to be carved from the Northwest Territory. The capital is Lansing. Michigan covers the largest area of any U.S. state east of the Mississippi River. Population (2010) 9,883,640; (2016 est.) 9,928,300.	
Minnesota	Minnesota became the 32nd state of the union on May 11, 1858. A small extension of the northern boundary makes Minnesota the most northerly of the 48 conterminous U.S. states. St. Paul is the state capital, and the Twin Cities region (Minneapolis–St. Paul) is the major administrative, economic, and cultural hub of Minnesota. Population (2010) 5,303,925; (2016 est.) 5,519,952.	
Mississippi	Mississippi derives from a Native American word meaning "great waters" or "father of waters." Mississippi became the 20th state of the union in 1817. Jackson is the state capital. Population (2010) 2,967,297; (2016 est.) 2,988,726.	
Missouri	Missouri was admitted as the 24th member of the union on August 10, 1821. The capital is Jefferson City. Missouri has some of the world's largest deposits of lead. Population (2010) 5,988,927; (2016 est.) 6,093,000.	
Montana	In 1889, Montana became the 41st state. Helena is the capital. Montana is called the Treasure State because of its immense mineral wealth. Population (2010) 989,415; (2016 est.) 1,042,520.	
Nebraska	Nebraska was admitted to the union as the 37th state on March 1, 1867. Lincoln is the capital. Nebraska was the first state in the country to celebrate Arbor Day—in 1872, when Nebraskan politician J. Sterling Morton advocated a tree-planting day to beautify the state's largely treeless landscape. Population (2010) 1,826,341; (2016 est.) 1,907,116.	
Nevada	Nevada became the 36th state of the union on October 31, 1864. It ranks seventh among the 50 U.S. states in terms of total area. It also, however, is one of the most sparsely settled. Carson City, in the western part of the state, is the capital. In 1950 Nevada was the state with the fewest people. By 2010, 15 states were smaller. Population (2010) 2,700,551; (2016 est.) 2,940,058.	
New Hampshire	New Hampshire was one of the 13 original U.S. states. It is located in New England at the extreme northeastern corner of the country. The capital is Concord. The first free public library in the world was founded in 1833 at Peterborough, New Hampshire. Population (2010) 1,316,470; (2016 est.) 1,334,795.	
New Jersey	New Jersey is one of the original 13 states. The capital is Trenton. New Jersey is called the Garden State because it became famous in the 18th century for the fertility of its land. It is now also among the most urbanized and crowded of states. Population (2010) 8,791,894; (2016 est.) 8,944,469.	
New Mexico	New Mexico became the 47th state of the union in 1912. The capital of New Mexico is Santa Fe, which was was founded in 1610 and is the oldest continuously used seat of government in North America. English novelist D.H. Lawrence lived in Taos in the early 1920s, and his ashes are buried there. Population (2010) 2,059,179; (2016 est.) 2,081,015.	

New York	New York is one of the 13 original states. The capital is Albany. Four U.S. presidents—Van Buren, Cleveland, and both Roosevelts—have been governor of New York. Population (2010) 19,378,102; (2016 est.) 19,745,289.	
North Carolina	North Carolina is one of the 13 original states. The capital is Raleigh. The Biltmore estate in Asheville, North Carolina, was the world's largest private house when built. Population (2010) 9,535,483; (2016 est.) 10,146,788.	
North Dakota	North Dakota was admitted to the union as the 39th state on Nov. 2, 1889. Bismarck, located in the centre of the state, is the capital. The North Dakota town of Rugby is considered to be the geographic center of the North American continent. Population (2010) 672,591; (2016 est.) 757,952.	
Ohio	The first state to be carved from the Northwest Territory, Ohio became the 17th member of the union on March 1, 1803. Ohio's capital, after being located in Chillicothe and Zanesville during the early years of statehood, was finally established in newly founded and centrally located Columbus in 1816. The five-sided Ohio flag is the only U.S. state flag that is not rectangular in shape. Population (2010) 11,536,504; (2016 est.) 11,614,373.	
Oklahoma	Since its admission in 1907 as the 46th state of the union, Oklahoma has achieved an integration of its Native American citizens into modern economic and social life that probably is unmatched by any other state. The capital is Oklahoma City, near the center of the state. Population (2010) 3,751,351; (2016 est.) 3,923,561.	
Oregon	Admitted to the union as the 33rd state on February 14, 1859, Oregon comprises an area of startling physical diversity, from the moist rainforests, mountains, and fertile valleys of its western third to the naturally arid and climatically harsh eastern deserts. The capital is Salem, in the northwestern part of the state. Pop. (2010) 3,831,074; (2016 est.) 4,093,465.	
Pennsylvania	Pennsylvania, officially Commonwealth of Pennsylvania, is one of the original 13 states. Harrisburg, nestled in the foothills of the Appalachian Mountains, is the capital. The worst nuclear accident in the United States happened in 1979 at Three Mile Island in Pennsylvania. Population (2010) 12,702,379; (2016 est.) 12,784,227.	
Rhode Island	Rhode Island, officially The State of Rhode Island and Providence Plantations, is one of the original 13 states and is one of the six New England states. The capital is Providence. Rhode Island's Flying Horse Merry-Go-Round, from 1876, is the oldest carousel in the United States. Population (2010) 1,052,567; (2016 est.) 1,056,426.	
South Carolina	South Carolina is one of the 13 states. Columbia, located in the center of the state, is the capital and largest city. The state experiences some 10 tornadoes a year, usually occurring during the spring. Tropical cyclones (hurricanes) are less frequent, but they do in some years cause damage to South Carolina's coast. Population (2010) 4,625,364; (2016 est.) 4,961,119.	
South Dakota	South Dakota became the 40th state of the union on November 2, 1889. Pierre, in central South Dakota, is one of the country's smallest state capitals. The Sturgis Motorcycle Rally, which dates from 1938, draws hundreds of thousands of bikers to the state each year to witness the Jackpine Gypsies Championship Half-Mile Race and to ride the roadways that snake through the Black Hills. Population (2010) 814,180; (2016 est.) 865,454.	

Tennessee	Tennessee is located in the upper South of the eastern United States and became the 16th state of the union in 1796. Nashville is the capital and Memphis the largest city. Reelfoot Lake in Tennessee was formed by major earthquakes that struck the area in the early 1800s. Population (2010) 6,346,105; (2016 est.) 6,651,194.	
Texas	Texas became the 28th state of the union in 1845. Texas occupies the south-central segment of the country and is the largest state in area except for Alaska. Austin, in the south-central part of the state, is the capital. "Texas" is the Spanish spelling of a Native American word meaning "friends" or "allies."Population (2010) 25,145,561; (2016 est.) 27,862,596.	
Utah	Utah became the 45th member of the union on January 4, 1896. The capital, Salt Lake City, is located in the north-central region of the state. In 1869, in Promontory, Utah, the first railroad to cross the United States was completed. Population (2010) 2,763,885; (2016 est.) 3,051,217.	
Vermont	Vermont is one of the six New England states lying in the northeastern corner of the country. It was admitted to the union on March 4, 1791, as the 14th state. It is sparsely populated, and its capital, Montpelier, is one of the least-populous U.S. state capitals. Vermont produces the most maple syrup in the United States. Population (2010) 625,741; (2016 est.) 624,594.	
Virginia	Virginia is one of the original 13 states. The state capital is Richmond. History and nature make Virginia a leading tourist centre. Within its borders lie many important historical monuments. Population (2010) 8,001,024; (2016 est.) 8,411,808.	
Washington	Washington was admitted into the union as the 42nd state in 1889. The capital is Olympia, located at the southern end of Puget Sound in the western part of the state. The state's coastal location and excellent harbors give it a leading role in trade with Alaska, Canada, and countries of the Pacific Rim. Pop. (2010) 6,724,540; (2016 est.) 7,288,000.	
West Virginia	West Virginia was admitted to the union as the 35th state in 1863. The state capital is Charleston. Forests cover more than three-fourths of the state. Population (2010) 1,852,994; (2016 est.) 1,831,102.	
Wisconsin	Wisconsin was admitted to the union as the 30th state on May 29, 1848. Madison, in south-central Wisconsin, is the state capital. In the southern two-thirds of the state, a combination of favorable climate, soil, and topography makes possible dairy agriculture that allows Wisconsin to be the top producer of cheese in the country and one of the top producers of milk and butter. Population (2010) 5,686,986; (2016 est.) 5,778,708.	
Wyoming	Wyoming became the 44th state of the Union on July 10, 1890. It ranks 10th among the 50 U.S. states in terms of total area. Cheyenne, the capital, is located in the southeastern corner of the state. Wyoming is home to Yellowstone National Park, which has the world's largest collection of geysers. Population (2010) 563,626; (2016 est.) 585,501.	

THE PRESIDENTS OF THE UNITED STATES

1	**George Washington**	George Washington, also called Father of His Country, (born February 22 [February 11, Old Style], 1732, Westmoreland county, Virginia [U.S.]—died December 14, 1799, Mount Vernon, Virginia, U.S.), American general and commander in chief of the colonial armies in the American Revolution (1775–83) and subsequently first president of the United States (1789–97).	
2	**John Adams**	John Adams, (born October 30 [October 19, Old Style], 1735, Braintree [now in Quincy], Massachusetts [U.S.]—died July 4, 1826, Quincy), early advocate of American independence from Great Britain, major figure in the Continental Congress (1774–77), first vice president (1789–97) and second president (1797–1801) of the United States.	
3	**Thomas Jefferson**	Thomas Jefferson, (born April 13 [April 2, Old Style], 1743, Shadwell, Virginia [U.S.]—died July 4, 1826, Monticello, Virginia, U.S.), draftsman of the Declaration of Independence of the United States and the nation's first secretary of state (1789–94), second vice president (1797–1801), and, as the third president (1801–09), the statesman responsible for the Louisiana Purchase.	
4	**James Madison**	James Madison, in full James Madison, Jr., (born March 16 [March 5, Old Style], 1751, Port Conway, Virginia [U.S.]—died June 28, 1836, Montpelier, Virginia, U.S.), fourth president of the United States (1809–17) and one of the Founding Fathers of his country.	
5	**James Monroe**	James Monroe, (born April 28, 1758, Westmoreland county, Virginia [U.S.]—died July 4, 1831, New York, New York, U.S.), fifth president of the United States (1817–25), who issued an important contribution to U.S. foreign policy in the Monroe Doctrine, a warning to European nations against intervening in the Western Hemisphere.	
6	**John Quincy Adams**	John Quincy Adams, byname Old Man Eloquent, (born July 11, 1767, Braintree [now Quincy], Massachusetts [U.S.]—died February 23, 1848, Washington, D.C., U.S.), eldest son of President John Adams and sixth president of the United States (1825–29).	
7	**Andrew Jackson**	Andrew Jackson, byname Old Hickory, (born March 15, 1767, Waxhaws region, South Carolina [U.S.]—died June 8, 1845, the Hermitage, near Nashville, Tennessee, U.S.), military hero and seventh president of the United States (1829–37).	
8	**Martin Van Buren**	Martin Van Buren, (born December 5, 1782, Kinderhook, New York, U.S.—died July 24, 1862, Kinderhook), eighth president of the United States (1837–41) and one of the founders of the Democratic Party.	
9	**William Henry Harrison**	William Henry Harrison, (born February 9, 1773, Charles City county, Virginia [U.S.]—died April 4, 1841, Washington, D.C., U.S.), ninth president of the United States (1841), whose Indian campaigns, while he was a territorial governor and army officer, thrust him into the national limelight and led to his election in 1840.	
10	**John Tyler**	John Tyler, (born March 29, 1790, Charles City county, Virginia, U.S.—died January 18, 1862, Richmond, Virginia, U.S.), 10th president of the United States (1841–45), who took office after Pres. William Henry Harrison died.	

11	**James K. Polk**	James K. Polk, in full James Knox Polk, (born November 2, 1795, Mecklenburg county, North Carolina, U.S.—died June 15, 1849, Nashville, Tennessee, U.S.), 11th president of the United States (1845–49). Under his leadership the United States fought the Mexican War (1846–48) and acquired vast territories along the Pacific coast and in the Southwest.	
12	**Zachary Taylor**	Zachary Taylor, (born November 24, 1784, Montebello plantation, near Gordonsville, Virginia, U.S.—died July 9, 1850, Washington, D.C., U.S.), 12th president of the United States (1849–50). Elected on the ticket of the Whig Party as a hero of the Mexican-American War (1846–48).	
13	**Millard Fillmore**	Millard Fillmore, (born January 7, 1800, Locke township, New York, U.S.—died March 8, 1874, Buffalo, New York, U.S.), 13th president of the United States (1850–53), whose insistence on federal enforcement of the Fugitive Slave Act of 1850 alienated the North and led to the destruction of the Whig Party.	
14	**Franklin Pierce**	Franklin Pierce, byname Young Hickory, (born November 23, 1804, Hillsboro, New Hampshire, U.S.—died October 8, 1869, Concord, New Hampshire, U.S.), 14th president of the United States (1853–57). He failed to deal effectively with the corroding sectional controversy over slavery in the decade preceding the American Civil War (1861–65).	
15	**James Buchanan**	James Buchanan, (born April 23, 1791, near Mercersburg, Pennsylvania, U.S.—died June 1, 1868, near Lancaster, Pennsylvania, U.S.), 15th president of the United States (1857–61), a moderate Democrat whose efforts to find a compromise in the conflict between the North and the South failed to avert the Civil War (1861–65).	
16	**Abraham Lincoln**	Abraham Lincoln, byname Honest Abe, the Rail-Splitter, or the Great Emancipator, (born February 12, 1809, near Hodgenville, Kentucky, U.S.—died April 15, 1865, Washington, D.C., U.S.), 16th president of the United States (1861–65), who preserved the Union during the American Civil War and brought about the emancipation of the slaves.	
17	**Andrew Johnson**	Andrew Johnson, (born December 29, 1808, Raleigh, North Carolina, U.S.—died July 31, 1875, near Carter Station, Tennessee, U.S.), 17th president of the United States (1865–69), who took office upon the assassination of Pres. Abraham Lincoln during the closing months of the American Civil War (1861–65).	
18	**Ulysses S. Grant**	Ulysses S. Grant, original name Hiram Ulysses Grant, (born April 27, 1822, Point Pleasant, Ohio, U.S.—died July 23, 1885, Mount McGregor, New York, U.S.), U.S. general, commander of the Union armies during the late years of the American Civil War, and 18th president of the United States (1869–77).	
19	**Rutherford B. Hayes**	Rutherford B. Hayes, in full Rutherford Birchard Hayes, (born October 4, 1822, Delaware, Ohio, U.S.—died January 17, 1893, Fremont, Ohio, U.S.), 19th president of the United States (1877–81), who brought post-Civil War Reconstruction to an end in the South and who tried to establish new standards of official integrity after eight years of corruption.	
20	**James A. Garfield**	James A. Garfield, in full James Abram Garfield, (born November 19, 1831, near Orange [in Cuyahoga county], Ohio, U.S.—died September 19, 1881, Elberon [now in Long Branch], New Jersey), 20th president of the United States (March 4–September 19, 1881), who had the second shortest tenure in presidential history after he was shot 4 months into office.	
21	**Chester A. Arthur**	Chester A. Arthur, in full Chester Alan Arthur, (born October 5, 1829, North Fairfield, Vermont, U.S.—died November 18, 1886, New York, New York), 21st president of the United States. Elected vice president on the Republican ticket of 1880, Arthur acceded to the presidency upon the assassination of President James A. Garfield.	

22 & 24	**Grover Cleveland**	Grover Cleveland, in full Stephen Grover Cleveland, (born March 18, 1837, Caldwell, New Jersey, U.S.—died June 24, 1908, Princeton, New Jersey), 22nd and 24th president of the United States (1885–89 and 1893–97) and the only president ever to serve two discontinuous terms.	
23	**Benjamin Harrison**	Benjamin Harrison, (born August 20, 1833, North Bend, Ohio, U.S.—died March 13, 1901, Indianapolis, Indiana), 23rd president of the United States (1889–93), a moderate Republican who won an electoral majority while losing the popular vote by more than 100,000 to Democrat Grover Cleveland.	
25	**William McKinley**	William McKinley, (born January 29, 1843, Niles, Ohio, U.S.—died September 14, 1901, Buffalo, New York), 25th president of the United States (1897–1901). Under McKinley's leadership, the United States went to war against Spain in 1898 and thereby acquired a global empire, including Puerto Rico, Guam, and the Philippines.	
26	**Theodore Roosevelt**	Theodore Roosevelt, bynames Teddy Roosevelt and TR, (born October 27, 1858, New York, New York, U.S.—died January 6, 1919, Oyster Bay, New York), the 26th president of the United States (1901–09) and a writer, naturalist, and soldier.	
27	**William Howard Taft**	William Howard Taft, (born September 15, 1857, Cincinnati, Ohio, U.S.—died March 8, 1930, Washington, D.C.), 27th president of the United States (1909–13) and 10th chief justice of the United States (1921–30).	
28	**Woodrow Wilson**	Woodrow Wilson, in full Thomas Woodrow Wilson, (born December 28, 1856, Staunton, Virginia, U.S.—died February 3, 1924, Washington, D.C.), 28th president of the United States (1913–21), an American scholar and statesman best remembered for his legislative accomplishments and his high-minded idealism.	
29	**Warren G. Harding**	Warren G. Harding, in full Warren Gamaliel Harding, (born November 2, 1865, Caledonia [now Blooming Grove], Ohio, U.S.—died August 2, 1923, San Francisco, California), 29th president of the United States (1921–23). He died his third year in office.	
30	**Calvin Coolidge**	Calvin Coolidge, in full John Calvin Coolidge, (born July 4, 1872, Plymouth, Vermont, U.S.—died January 5, 1933, Northampton, Massachusetts), 30th president of the United States (1923–29). Coolidge acceded to the presidency after the death in office of Warren G. Harding.	
31	**Herbert Hoover**	Herbert Hoover, in full Herbert Clark Hoover, (born August 10, 1874, West Branch, Iowa, U.S.—died October 20, 1964, New York, New York), 31st president of the United States (1929–33). Hoover's reputation as a humanitarian—earned during and after World War I as he rescued millions of Europeans from starvation—faded from public consciousness when his administration proved unable to alleviate the pain of the Great Depression.	
32	**Franklin D. Roosevelt**	Franklin D. Roosevelt, in full Franklin Delano Roosevelt, byname FDR, (born January 30, 1882, Hyde Park, New York, U.S.—died April 12, 1945, Warm Springs, Georgia), 32nd president of the United States (1933–45). The only president elected to the office four times, he led the country through the Great Depression and World War II.	
33	**Harry S. Truman**	Harry S. Truman, (born May 8, 1884, Lamar, Missouri, U.S.—died December 26, 1972, Kansas City, Missouri), 33rd president of the United States (1945–53), who led his country through the final stages of World War II and through the early years of the Cold War.	
34	**Dwight D. Eisenhower**	Dwight D. Eisenhower, in full Dwight David Eisenhower, (born October 14, 1890, Denison, Texas, U.S.—died March 28, 1969, Washington, D.C.), 34th president of the United States (1953–61), who had been supreme commander of the Allied forces in western Europe during World War II.	

35	John F. Kennedy	John F. Kennedy, in full John Fitzgerald Kennedy, byname JFK, (born May 29, 1917, Brookline, Massachusetts, U.S.—died November 22, 1963, Dallas, Texas), 35th president of the United States (1961–63), who faced a number of foreign crises, especially in Cuba and Berlin, but managed to secure such achievements as the Nuclear Test-Ban Treaty and the Alliance for Progress.	
36	Lyndon B. Johnson	Lyndon B. Johnson, in full Lyndon Baines Johnson, also called LBJ, (born August 27, 1908, Gillespie county, Texas, U.S.—died January 22, 1973, San Antonio, Texas), 36th president of the United States (1963–69). A moderate Democrat and vigorous leader in the United States Senate, Johnson acceded to the presidency in 1963 upon the assassination of President John F. Kennedy.	
37	Richard Nixon	Richard Nixon, in full Richard Milhous Nixon, (born January 9, 1913, Yorba Linda, California, U.S.—died April 22, 1994, New York, New York), 37th president of the United States (1969–74), who, faced with almost certain impeachment for his role in the Watergate scandal, became the first American president to resign from office.	
38	Gerald Ford	Gerald Ford, in full Gerald Rudolph Ford, Jr., original name Leslie Lynch King, Jr., (born July 14, 1913, Omaha, Nebraska, U.S.—died December 26, 2006, Rancho Mirage, California), 38th president of the United States (1974–77), who, as 40th vice president, succeeded to the presidency on the resignation of President Richard M. Nixon.	
39	Jimmy Carter	Jimmy Carter, in full James Earl Carter, Jr., (born October 1, 1924, Plains, Georgia, U.S.), 39th president of the United States (1977–81), who served as the nation's chief executive during a time of serious problems at home and abroad.	
40	Ronald Reagan	Ronald Reagan, in full Ronald Wilson Reagan, (born February 6, 1911, Tampico, Illinois, U.S.—died June 5, 2004, Los Angeles, California), 40th president of the United States (1981–89), noted for his conservative Republicanism, his fervent anticommunism, and his appealing personal style, characterized by a jaunty affability and folksy charm.	
41	George H. W. Bush	George H.W. Bush, in full George Herbert Walker Bush, (born June 12, 1924, Milton, Massachusetts, U.S.), politician and businessman who was vice president of the United States (1981–89) and the 41st president of the United States (1989–93).	
42	Bill Clinton	Bill Clinton, byname of William Jefferson Clinton, original name William Jefferson Blythe III, (born August 19, 1946, Hope, Arkansas, U.S.), 42nd president of the United States (1993–2001), who oversaw the country's longest peacetime economic expansion.	
43	George W. Bush	George W. Bush, in full George Walker Bush, (born July 6, 1946, New Haven, Connecticut, U.S.), 43rd president of the United States (2001–09), who led his country's response to the September 11 terrorist attacks in 2001 and initiated the Iraq War in 2003.	
44	Barack Obama	Barack Obama, in full Barack Hussein Obama II, (born August 4, 1961, Honolulu, Hawaii, U.S.), 44th president of the United States (2009–17) and the first African American to hold the office.	
45	Donald Trump	Donald Trump, in full Donald John Trump, (born June 14, 1946, New York, New York, U.S.), 45th president of the United States (2017–). Trump was also a real-estate developer who amassed vast hotel, casino, and other real-estate properties in the New York City area and around the world.	